HANDBOOK

ON

POPULATION

FIFTH EDITION

BY

ROBERT L. SASSONE

The author's special thanks for assistance to Lucy Brown, Joseph Damroth, Robert Lynch, Jamie Akana, Susan Morriss, Elizabeth Ruth, Robert Louis and Holly Sassone

PREFACE

> You see things; and you say, "Why?" But I dream
> things that never were; and I say "Why not?"
>
> George Bernard Shaw
> *Back to Methuselah*
> pt. 1, Act 1, 1921

UNICEF alleges that nearly 3 million of the 12.9 million annual child deaths could be prevented by 25 cents per child worth of cotrimoxazole. (SW4) Many other deaths could be prevented at low cost. The author asks: "Why not?" Why not make more progress in reducing the number of deaths of young children? Why not solve a lot of other problems?

The prevailing answers are: "because we have to stop population growth first," "because it's too costly" or "because there is not enough of this or too much of that." Things there are alleged to be not enough of relate to population and include food, resources, energy, ozone, quality of life, and space. Things there are alleged to be too much of include pollution, species extinction, global warming, ultraviolet radiation, people, and population growth.

Many of the excuses for not saving the 3 million children derive from arguments that we must first stop population growth. (WC)

This book examines population growth to determine if it is a severe problem, as many believe, or if we should worry less about it and switch our efforts to problems like preventing the deaths of those 3 million children.

REFERENCES:

(SW) *The State of the World's Children 1993* United Nations International Children's Emergency Fund (UNICEF)

(WC) President Clinton to UN General Assembly: "To ensure a healthier and more abundant world, we simply must slow the world's explosive growth in population." as quoted by US Ambassador Victor Marrero, in the Second Committee, on Agenda Item #96, the International Conference on Population and Development, 11/4/93. This speech, like too many others, repeatedly indicated population growth as the problem we must solve, but ignored development and reducing unnecessary deaths.

FORMAT

A question-and-answer format is used to help the reader to quickly find desired facts. References are at the end of each chapter for easy accessibility. Footnotes usually comprise two capital letters in parentheses, sometimes followed by a page number or other indication of how to find desired data within the reference.

Other steps are taken to save space. For additional details or updated references, please contact ALL, P.O. 1350, Stafford, VA 22555, (703) 659-4171. Send $4 to ALL to purchase a book.

Telephone numbers of references permitting the reader to obtain additional information from the author's references or a way to obtain the numbers will usually be given on request. Requested referenced material will usually be sent without charge to those sending a stamped self-addressed envelope with their request.

TABLE OF CONTENTS

CHAPTER 1

UNDERSTANDING POPULATION

101 What does this book do?

Population control advocates and their opponents make contradictory claims about the population situation. This book gives the reader enough facts to determine which side is to be believed.

102 What is the population controversy?

Population control activists and supporters say that there are either too many people now or that there will be soon. These activists say that overpopulation is so severe that governments must impose population control. Others disagree with the population control activists and oppose this sort of government intervention.

For example, UNICEF estimates that 12.9 million children die annually. Population control advocates blame the deaths on an inability to grow enough food for a growing population. They allege that nothing can be done to prevent these deaths until we first reduce population growth, so that the best way to prevent deaths is to spend billions of dollars on family planning.

Population control opponents counter that there is plenty of food and claim most of the deaths could be prevented by a variety of cost-effective techniques. They cite particular examples like the UNICEF claim that more than one million deaths from pneumonia could be prevented annually at a cost of 25 cents per child for cotrimoxazole, an antibiotic, plus a distribution cost. (SW4)

103 What is population control?

Population control is use of government money, laws, incentives and force to control conduct and persuade or force people to have fewer children. Population control is the use of government and media by a few to tell everyone else how many can live.

104 Why is it so important to determine which side is correct about population?

Advocates of population control allege that population growth has caused and will continue to cause problems so serious that drastic action must be taken to stop population growth. Activists use population growth as a reason to coerce changes in people's intimate beliefs and childbearing practices. These activists also use population control arguments that attack traditional moral and family values.

105 Why can it be argued that traditional Christianity's belief about population is wrong if the population controllers are correct?

Traditional Christianity claims to be a religion revealed by God, not just a mere philosophy. If God is infallible and truly founded Christianity, Christianity could not make a major error. Genesis 1:28 states: "God blessed them, saying: 'Be fertile and multiply; fill the earth and subdue it'" (New American Bible). All Christian churches condemned all forms of abortion and artificial birth control (condoms, etc.) for 1900 years until about 1930. Even today, churches to which most Christians in the world belong condemn all but natural family planning. If the population controllers are correct, it can be argued that Christianity is wrong because its teachings cause more babies to be born.

106 How do advocates of population control describe the population situation?

"The U.S. hopes that the document [to be prepared by the 1994 UN Population Conference in Cairo] will state clearly that stabilizing the world's population is a goal which underlies and mutually reinforces all of the other goals that have already been identified." (VM)

"Our runaway brain has enabled us to multiply unreasonably in numbers, putting such pressures on the planet that ecological and nuclear catastrophes become a real possibility. . . . Surely we are too smart to go on breeding ourselves to extinction, destroying most of the rest of the species on the planet in the process." (DI)

107 What reasons do population control advocates give for their conclusion that the earth is overpopulated?

Population control advocates allege that overpopulation has caused the following problems:

a) Food shortages—"The world will undergo famines-hundreds of millions of people are going to starve to death in spite of any crash programs embarked upon now." (PB, Prologue)

b) Resource depletion—They claim that we will run out of important minerals such as uranium, manganese, chromium, nickel, zinc, tin, aluminum, gold, silver, platinum, and lead. (PR, PE, G2)

c) Energy shortages—They claim that more people use more energy and will cause us to run out of petroleum, natural gas and coal. (PR, PE, G2)

d) Overcrowding now—Population control advocates claim that even today there is not enough available space per person.

e) Massive overcrowding soon—Since there is only a limited amount of space, and population has apparently doubled every given number of years, population control advocates claim that population must inevitably overcrowd everywhere.

f) Deteriorating quality of life. (PE, PB, LG, G2)

g) Pollution— They claim that increased population growth necessarily means increased pollution, so much so that it could lead to global extermination. (LG)

h) Severe global warming—Increased population and more energy use cause more carbon dioxide to be released into the atmosphere. Population control advocates allege that this will cause disastrous global warming.

i) Ozone depletion—Population control advocates allege that more people result in more chemical pollution that destroys more atmospheric ozone, allowing more ultraviolet light to reach the earth and causing millions to die from skin cancer.

j) Massive extinction—Population control advocates allege that the increase in numbers of people is crowding the earth so much that many thousands of species become extinct each year.

3

k) Literally the end of the world as we know it. The combination of problems caused by population growth may destroy the world, since they cannot be solved with only our limited assets. (LG)

l) Finally, population control advocates allege that there is no advantage to additional population growth. According to them, even if we are not sure that disasters will follow, there is no reason to permit continued population growth.

108 How do opponents of population control respond to claims by population control advocates?

There are about fifty ways to test claims made by population control advocates. Later chapters of this book examine and use these fifty or so tests. Opponents of population control allege that fair interpretation of the facts shows that every argument for population control is frivolous.

109 Is there a general rule for finding which side of this controversy is correct?

In a complicated controversy, a good way to learn which side is telling the truth is to look at the content of opposing arguments.

The side that is incorrect often repeats simple statements supporting their position and avoids mentioning arguments by the opposition. *This side hopes to win by keeping you in the dark about opposition arguments.*

By contrast, the side that is correct will not shy away from mentioning opposing arguments to show why they are incorrect or not relevant. *They hope to win because you know the opposition arguments but know why they are incorrect.*

110 What are tests that can be used to catch the side that is lying?

First break down big questions into simpler component parts. Then compare the facts by applying these rules.

a) Which side states facts that more closely explain the known situation?

b) Which side gives the information that negates the opposing side's claims?

c) Which side gives and repeats only partial explanations?

d) Which side suppresses unfavorable facts?

e) Which side makes wrong predictions?

f) Which side relies on statements that cannot be proven?

111 How many of the major statements of the advocates of population control were incorrect when made or have been proven incorrect in recent years?

Opponents of population control allege that all major statements allegedly justifying population control are false. This book discusses the most important of these disputed statements.

4

112 Name the foremost pro-population control study, book and individuals.

The most important U.S. Government study favoring population control has been the 1980 *Global 2000 Report to the President* by the Carter administration. The most important non-government study has been *Limits to Growth* by Meadows, et al. The most famous individual advocate of population control has been Stanford Professor Paul Ehrlich, who wrote the most publicized book *Population Bomb*. Their arguments are still honored and respected by population control advocates. For example, on September 20, 1993, Jane Fonda made a pro-population control speech to the United Nations in which she favorably cited both Meadows and Ehrlich.

113 How accurate were the data, methods, predictions and conclusions of *Global 2000*?

The data of *Global 2000* were incomplete and inaccurate in most essential areas related to its conclusions about population. The predictions and conclusions of *Global 2000* were not accurate and did not follow from the data. They apparently were selected to mislead rather than inform. A typical prediction claimed that due to shortages, U.S. gasoline prices would be $3 per gallon before 1993. *Global 2000* omitted contradictory data. Its summaries and conclusions, given massive publicity, did not follow from its data. For a detailed analysis of *Global 2000* and its many errors and misleading statements, please see *The Resourceful Earth: A Response to Global 2000* (1984), edited by Simon and Kahn.

114 How accurate were the data, methods, predictions and conclusions of *Limits to Growth*?

Limits to Growth was the most famous computer study alleging that population growth should be stopped. It predicted that the world would come to an end with the death of all humans within 100 years (by about 2070) if population growth continued.

The data of *Limits to Growth* were incomplete and sometimes inaccurate. Additionally, the leader of *Limits to Growth* admitted that they had deliberately lied in order to jolt people into accepting their desired conclusions. (TI) Contrary data that should have been considered were omitted.

Limits to Growth's methods were likewise flawed. In one of the major calculation factors there was an error of 900%. If this is corrected, *Limits to Growth* comes to very different, non-threatening conclusions, and the world does not come to an end. (NA)

The rules used in *Limits to Growth* included an assumption that there would be no substantial scientific or technical advances. In the real world, scientific and technical advances are consistently increasing in number and importance. As a demonstration of the

5

significance of its error, these rules were used to predict the period 1870 to 1970 from the basis of what was known in 1870, and the computer calculated that the world had to come to an end before 1970, in part because of the inability to control the massive amounts of horse manure.

115 How accurate have the predictions of individual population control advocates been?

The following are taken from the 1968 *Population Bomb* by Paul Ehrlich.

a) "The next nine years [ending in 1977] will probably tell the story." p 21

b) "The battle to feed all of humanity is over. In the 1970's the world will undergo famines-hundreds of millions of people are going to starve to death in spite of any crash programs embarked upon now." (Prologue)

c) "At this late date nothing can prevent a substantial increase in the world death rate." (Prologue)

d) "Each year food production in underdeveloped countries falls a bit further behind burgeoning population growth, and people go to bed a little bit hungrier." (p 17)

e) "A minimum of 3½ million will starve to death this year, mostly children. But this is a mere handful compared to the numbers that will be starving in a decade or so." (p 17)

f) "The world, especially the undeveloped world, is rapidly running out of food" (p 36). Compare the preceding statements about food with the food data in Chapter 2 of this book. *Population Bomb* contained no specific statements about resources that could be checked. Ehrlich did, however make specific statements about resources in *Population, Resources, Environment*, published in 1970, as follows:

g) The U.S. should by now have run out of reserves of crude oil, uranium, manganese, cobalt, copper, chromium, nickel, lead, zinc, tin, aluminum, gold, silver and platinum.

h) The world should have already run out of each of the following minerals: lead, zinc, tin, gold, silver, platinum, and should run out of natural gas, copper and tungsten about the year 2000, and crude oil shortly thereafter.

The preceding statements about resources should be compared with the resource data in chapter 3 of this book.

116 How accurate were the population controller predictions?

a) The world food situation improved by an average of 1% per year every year of the 20 years before 1968, the year Ehrlich wrote *Population Bomb*. Ehrlich did not mention this 20% improvement. In the nine years after *Population Bomb* was written, a time which Ehrlich claimed would be critical, every prediction about food made by Ehrlich was proven wrong.

Furthermore, the trends improved and went opposite of the way he said. Food production in the years since *Population Bomb* has continued to increase faster than population has increased. (SFv)

b) In the 1970's there were no major famines. The rate of starvation has probably been at least a thousand times lower than predicted by Ehrlich. In the most famous 1970's famine, in the Sahel, according to relief workers on the scene, the only human deaths were caused by the failure of people to go to where relief supplies were being distributed. There was always sufficient food available. According to UN data, there was no significant increase in the death rate in any nation affected by the famine. There was more grain carried over in storage inside the nations affected by the famine than there had been ten years before the famine. The famine was not significant enough to reduce population growth in the affected nations. (If there had been substantial famine deaths, population would have declined.)

c) There has not been any increase in the world death rate. In fact, there has been a substantial reduction in the death rate and an increase in life expectancy averaging at least four months longer life expectancy each year nearly everywhere. (DYv)

d) When made, Ehrlich's statement that food production was falling behind needs was exactly opposite to the truth. Each year since Ehrlich wrote *Population Bomb* in 1968, on the average, food production in developing countries has increased more than population growth. In fact, between the year *Population Bomb* was written and 1990, the average diet in developing nations, according to the UN, improved by 20%. Before 1968, according to the UN, fewer than 5% of people in developing nations lived in nations where the average diet exceeded 2,600 calories per day, while during 1987-1989, half the people in developing nations lived in nations where the average diet exceeded 2,600 calories per day. The U.S. government recommendation for average calorie intake is 2,200 calories per day. By 1990, developing countries inhabited by about 86% of people exceeded this amount, while most of the remaining 14% of people lived in countries where the average diet was just slightly below the recommended 2,200 calories per day. (SF91, pp 221-223)(FN)

e) Ehrlich's statement about starvation was wrong, exactly the opposite of what had been happening and exactly the opposite of what would happen since.

f) Ehrlich was wrong and apparently knew it. In the later editions of *Population Bomb*, published when people could determine there was no widespread starvation during the 1970s, Ehrlich changed his prediction to state: "In the 1970's and 1980's, the world will undergo famines-hundreds of millions of people are going to starve

7

to death in spite of any crash programs embarked upon now." His weakened prediction was still wrong; the food situation continued to improve.

g) Ehrlich was wrong about running out of minerals and energy. Reserves of energy and of nearly every mineral are at record high levels. Population control advocates intentionally misstate the mineral situation by not carefully explaining what reserves are. Reserves are the minerals that we know about that are cheapest to take out of the ground. They are used first because there is more profit in using them first. The total amount of a particular mineral may be billions of times greater than reserves.

117 What have advocates of population stagnation said about human rights?

Here are some quotes from Ardrey, Hardin, Harper, and Ehrlich.

"Humanism's respect for the dignity of man and its regard for every human life as sacred, while among the most powerful forces ever to advance man's welfare along certain fronts, had ambiguous results on others . . ." "We must consider enforced contraception, whether through taxation on surplus children, or through more severe means such as conception license, replacing or supplementing the marriage license. Abortion should be freely available to those suffering unintended pregnancy. In international relations, of course, any aid to peoples who through ignorance, prejudice or political hypnosis fail to control their numbers might be forbidden." (LI)

"If we love the truth we must openly deny the validity of the Universal Declaration of Human Rights, even though it is promoted by the United Nations." "As a genetically trained biologist . . . It seems to me that, if there are to be differences in individual inheritance, legal possession should be perfectly correlated with biological inheritance - that those who are biologically more fit to be the custodians of property should legally inherit more." "Coercion is a dirty word to most liberals now, but it need not forever be so. As with the four letter words, its dirtiness can be cleaned away by exposure to the light, by saying it over and over without apology or embarrassment." (GH)

"Effecting radical changes in the birth rates by voluntary means alone is 'manifestly hopeless,' Robert A. Harper of Washington told the American Psychological Association meeting here. . . . The only solution is to take away the right to reproduce, he said. . . . His recommendation would simply 'in one full and nondiscriminatory sweep take away the right to reproduce from everyone.'" (RH)

"Many of my colleagues feel that some sort of compulsory birth regulation would be necessary to achieve such control. One plan often mentioned involves the addition of temporary sterilants to the water supplies or staple food. Doses of antidote would be carefully rationed by the government to produce the desired population size." (PB135)

"A Federal Department of Population and Environment (DPE) should be set up with power to take whatever steps are necessary to establish a reasonable population size in the United States and to put an end to the steady deterioration of our environment. The DPE would be given ample funds to support research in the areas of population control and environmental quality. In the first area it would promote intensive investigation of new techniques of birth control, possibly leading to the development of mass sterilizing agents such as were discussed above." (PB138)

118 What apparently motivates population control leaders?

The author believes population explosion propaganda is used to deceive the public to justify political decisions that some population control leaders want made for other reasons.

REFERENCES

(DI)   *Discover* magazine, Aug, 1993, p 59
(DY)   *UN Demographic Yearbook*, published annually
(FN)   Source for the recommendation of 2,200 calories per person per day is the Food & Nutrition Board, National Academy of Sciences–National Research Council, which lists calories per person for various ages and both sexes; 2,200 calories is the average sufficient for the recommended age and sex calorie consumption
(G2)   *Global 2000 Report to the President*, Carter administration 1980
(GH)   Garrett Hardin, "The Tragedy of the Commons," *Science*, Dec 13, 1968
(LG)   D. H. Meadows, et al., *The Limits to Growth: A Report for the Club of Rome's Project on the Predicament of Mankind* Universe Books, NY (1972)
(LI)   Robert Ardrey, "Control of Population," *Life*, Feb 20, 1970
(NA)   *Nature* magazine, Sept 21, 1973
(PB)   Paul Ehrlich, *Population Bomb* (1968), Ballantine Books, NY
(PE)   Paul Ehrlich and Anne Ehrlich, *Population Explosion* (1990), Simon & Schuster, NY
(PR)   Paul Ehrlich, et al., *Population, Resources, Environment* (1970)
(RH)   *Ob.Gyn. News*, Nov 1, 1969
(SF)   *The State of Food & Agriculture*, published annually by the Food & Agricultural Organization of the United Nations. Year is the first two-digit number, followed by the page number. The term "v" means various and is used where various years contain the data
(SW)   *The State of the World's Children 1993*, published for UNICEF by Oxford University Press
(TI)   *Time* magazine, Apr 26, 1976, p 56
(VM)   Statement by U.S. Ambassador Victor Marrero to UN General Assembly, in the Second Committee, on Agenda Item #96, the International Conference on Population and Development, Nov 4, 1993

CHAPTER 2

FOOD PRODUCTION

201 What do advocates of population control say about food?
202 How do opponents criticize the statements population controllers make about food?
203 What do opponents of population control say about food?
204 How can you determine if the advocates or opponents of population control are correct about food?
205 What is the key thing to understand about food?
206 How many people die annually from starvation?
207 Why are the claims of malnutrition deaths by population controllers false?
208 What does the World Bank say about malnutrition?
209 Why is the World Bank malnutrition data in Q 208 misleading?
210 What are the leading causes of starvation?
211 Are large populations or high population density associated with malnutrition?
212 What is the leading cause, other than war, of child malnutrition?
213 Does government discrimination against agriculture substantially reduce food production?
214 Has world food production increased faster than population has grown?
215 What are the exact numbers showing food supply production per capita improvement since 1948?
216 How has the average diet in developing countries improved in calories consumed per day from the years 1961 to 1989?
217 How many developing countries have improved their per caput food production during the years of record population growth since 1948-1952?
218 What is the recommended number of calories which should be consumed each day?
219 In how many countries have people improved the average diet by increasing the number of calories consumed?
220 Has food production in the developing countries increased faster than population has grown?
221 How have cereal and meat production increased?
222 What is the most common technique population control advocates use to mislead the public?
223 How has production of grain, wheat, rice and meat increased in comparison with population?
224 Why has food production increased faster than population has grown in recent years?
225 Why is food production likely to increase faster than population growth in the developing countries in the future?

226 What has the UN said about how much of the world's arable land has been in use?

227 How much potential agricultural land is there in the world?

228 People of how many of the most populated developing countries consume enough calories?

229 How accurate are the assertions of Planned Parenthood about the world food situation?

230 How costly would it be to produce a machine that would prevent malnutrition?

201 What do advocates of population control say about food?

Advocates of population control have repeatedly claimed that a lack of food is the most important reason for population control. For example, "The most pressing factor now limiting the capacity of the earth to support Homo Sapiens is the supply of food." (PR66) "... it seems likely that food will be our limiting resource." (PE66)

202 How do opponents criticize the statements population controllers make about food?

Opponents allege that population controllers rely only on selected parts of UN and U.S. agriculture data, which, out of context, support their position. The overall data do not support their position.

Perhaps the best example of this is the annual report by Worldwatch Institute. In spite of many years of massive generally continual improvement in the world food situation, each January the Worldwatch Institute press release ignores the improvements. Instead, it finds some isolated thing somewhere in the world that has deteriorated, and focuses exclusively on what bad news there is. Much of the media each year reports the tiny misleading area described by the Worldwatch press release as if it were a fair description of the world food situation.

203 What do opponents of population control say about food?

Opponents of population control claim to rely on complete UN and U.S. food production and consumption data, which they allege shows that by every reasonable way to measure, the food situation has improved during the past 50 years of fast population growth. Food shortages and related problems such as malnutrition have diminished. In fact, food production could be increased so much, if desired, that potential food production should be no excuse for any human malnutrition.

204 How can you determine if the advocates or opponents of population control are correct about food?

If the advocates of population control are correct about food, then all the following statements should be false. If opponents of population control are correct, all the following statements should be true:

a) The amount of food produced per person has improved.

b) The average amount of calories eaten per person per day has increased.

c) The inhabitants of more countries eat sufficient numbers of calories than in previous years.

d) The percentage of people living in nations with poor diets has decreased and the percentage of people living in nations with sufficient diets has increased.

e) The amount of meat eaten per person has increased.

f) There are reasons to expect additional increases in yield.

g) Food is being grown on a relatively small fraction of all possible food-growing land.

h) The nations with the largest populations are feeding their people well.

i) Food problems are more likely in nations with fewer people.

j) People in nearly all nations have an improving and, on average, adequate diet.

k) Life expectancy is increasing substantially as population increases.

The more of the preceding a-k that are wrong, the more likely advocates of population control are correct. The more of the preceding a-k are correct, the more likely the opponents of population control are correct and the more likely it is that population growth is not a problem requiring population control.

205 What is the key thing to understand about food?

All of the statements a-k in the preceding question are true. The world food situation has been the best in world history during the generally continual improvement since 1948. Every year for about fifty years, the best description of the world food situation has been that recent years have been the best ever. There is no reason to expect that this improvement in the food situation will stop in the foreseeable future.

206 How many people die annually from starvation?

Nobody knows. The UN and the U.S. do not publish such data. Most starvation occurs in war zones where it is impossible to collect precise data.

207 Why are the claims of malnutrition deaths by population controllers false?

In 1968, Paul Ehrlich claimed that "In the 1970's the world will undergo famines—hundreds of millions of people are going to starve to death in spite of any crash programs embarked upon now." (PB) In later editions of his book, when it was obvious massive starvation was not occurring, Ehrlich changed the prediction from "In the 1970's" to "In the 1970's and 1980's." In the sequel to *Population Bomb, Population Explosion*, published in 1990, the third sentence of the Preface states, "Since 1968, at least 200 million people—mostly children—have perished needlessly of hunger and hunger-related diseases . . ." Ehrlich then references UNICEF, WHO, and "other sources" and claims in a footnote that "40,000 children [in the developing world] die daily (14.6 million a year) from hunger-related diseases . . . "

Via telephone, UNICEF strongly denied Ehrlich's claim that UNICEF ever said anything that could be interpreted to mean that 40,000 children in the developing world die daily from hunger-related diseases. UNICEF's spokesman and their publication *The State of the World's Children 1993* both stated, "The total number of child deaths in the developing world is given as 12.9 million." (SW1)

UNICEF reports 12.9 million children die annually from all causes, of which 8.1 million are preventable. Of these, 3.6 million are from pneumonia, 3 million from diarrhoeal diseases, 2.1 million from vaccine-preventable diseases, and 4.3 million from all other causes (some deaths have two causes). Death caused by malnutrition is not listed as a separate category, but more than 70% of the child deaths (SW70) are in countries where the average number of calories consumed exceeds what the U.S. recommends for a healthy diet. (FN)

208 What does the World Bank say about malnutrition?

"Low height for a given age, or stunting, is the most prevalent symptom of protein-energy malnutrition; approximately 40% of all two-year-olds in developing countries are short for their age" (WD 75). ". . . in developing countries 25% of those [child] deaths are attributed to mild or moderate underweight." (WD p 76 Table 4.3)

209 Why is the World Bank malnutrition data in Q 208 misleading?

The following examples of misleading World Bank statements discussed herein are typical.

Some of any group will be shorter. It is no surprise that 40% of children are short. The important question is whether this shortness is caused by malnutrition or some other cause such as an inherited tendency to be short. The World Bank data appears to be selected to mislead. Table 28 claims that 13% of Egyptian children under five are malnourished. (WD p 292) This appears misleading since Egyptians consume more calories than inhabitants of Great Britain, Canada or Australia, which have no reported child malnourishment problem. (SF92, pp 255-258)

In another example of misleading data (one out of many possible examples), in Table 28 the World Bank claims that 45% of Sri Lankan children under five are malnourished. (WD292) This appears unlikely, since according to the UNFAO, the average number of calories consumed in Sri Lanka for a generation (SF92 P256) has exceeded the 2,200 daily calorie intake recommended (FN) by the U.S. (SF92 p 256) UNICEF states that the Sri Lanka diet is greater than 100% of requirements. (SF71) Additional reasons for doubting the World Bank claim include the fact that Sri Lanka has a life expectancy greater than 70, which is unlikely if 45% of its children are malnourished. Sri Lanka had average 1991 life expectancy and a 1991 infant mortality rate better than some European countries. (SW69)

Many other examples can be given that cast additional doubt on the World Bank report's accuracy and honesty. Examining their definition of malnutrition, we find that it includes fat as well as thin children, and those who could benefit from a vitamin pill containing vitamin A, iron and iodine. (WD Table 28 explanation) In Table 4.3, they state that more than 70% of alleged malnutrition is caused by Vitamin A, iodine or iron deficiency. (WD76) The World Bank omits to state that this deficiency could be cleared up by a twice-a-week vitamin pill, total cost of about one dollar per year per child, assuming a cost of a penny per pill.

210 What are the leading causes of starvation?

Starvation is either death due to lack of food or death by causes stemming from a previous lack of food. There has been some starvation, but substantially all of that starvation has been caused by bad government.

War, including the use of food as a weapon, has been the greatest cause of starvation, responsible for perhaps as much as 90% of starvation deaths over the past 30 years. The list of countries with very poor diets contains nearly all the countries recently ravaged by war and few that have not been ravaged by war. (SF92 pp 255-257)

Inept government meddling with the economy, interfering with the incentive and opportunity for farmers to grow vast amounts of food, has been a great cause of lower food production leading to malnutrition, as discussed in Q212. Drought and bad weather occasionally reduce food production, but if a country has previously taken reasonable steps to encourage food production, past surpluses and imported food permit all to eat. Poverty and lack of transportation also contribute to malnutrition.

The assumption that all people who die underweight are killed by a lack of calories or protein is not true. Many diseases, such as diarrhoeal diseases and cancer, cause their victims to lose weight before death, regardless of food availability. (SW4-7, 12, 22, 34, 68-79)

211 Are large populations or high population density associated with malnutrition?

Large populations are not associated with malnutrition. The UNFAO lists the 20 countries having the worst food situation, and all of them are low-population countries. None of them are among the 20 most populous countries. 90% of them have below-average population densities. (SF92 p 24)

14

212 What is the leading cause, other than war, of child malnutrition?

UNICEF lists diarrhoeal diseases, not lack of food, as perhaps the major cause of malnutrition among the developing world's children. (SW22) Other causes of malnutrition include lack of vitamin A, iron and iodine, all of which could be prevented by a pill, given twice a week, at a cost of a penny a pill, adding up to a cost of about one dollar per year per child saved. Poverty sometimes makes the victim unable to purchase food. Lack of available food for those able to purchase it is seldom a cause. (SW4-7, 12, 22, 34, 68-79)

213 Does government discrimination against agriculture substantially reduce food production?

Yes. Norman Borloug, Nobel Peace Prize winner for his work with new seeds, stated at the UN Population Conference in 1984 that developing countries could double or triple their food production in 1985 if two reforms were instituted: fair credit for farmers, and fair prices for farmers.

The UNFAO stated, "It is by now commonly acknowledged that both economy-wide and sector-specific policies in many developing countries have discriminated against agriculture, resulting in a negative environment for agricultural production and investment opportunities." The article then went on to claim that food production would increase if countries were fair to their farmers. (SF90 p 94) Many developing countries discriminate against their farmers because they want to keep food prices low in the capital to reduce the risk of revolution.

214 Has world food production increased faster than population has grown?

Yes. There was only slight improvement in the food supply before about 1948, the year of the first UN data, which were slightly improved over the pre-World War II League of Nations data. Since 1948, there has been a more or less continual improvement of nearly one percent per year, so the amount of food per person produced and eaten in recent years by inhabitants of developing countries has been about 40% more than at any time before 1948. (SFv)

215 What are the exact numbers showing food supply production per capita improvement since 1948?

In an average year, world food production has increased more than 2% while population has increased less than 2%. The best measure of food supply per person is per caput (per person) food production. The UN only publishes recent years, so to obtain a long-term comparison, one must compare data from more than one edition of *The State of Food and Agriculture*. The exact data are as follows:

Per Caput (Per Person) World Food Production

	1986	1987	1988	1989	1990	1991
1979-81 average = 100						
World	105	103	103	105	106	103
Developing Countries	109	108	111	112	113	113
(SF92)						

	1980	1981	1982	1983	1984	1985
World	99	100	102	101	104	105
Developing Countries	99	102	103	104	107	108
(SF86)						

1969-71 average = 100					
	1977	1978	1979	1980	1981
World	104	107	106	104	105
Developing Countries	105	108	108	108	110
(SF82)					

years	1948-1952	1953-1957	1960	1965	1970
1952-56 average = 100					
World	93	101	107	108	112
Developing Countries	94	101	104	104	106
(SF58,66,70)					

Using the above data, the reader can verify that world per capita food production in 1989-1991 improved by 32% compared to the years 1948-1952, and developing countries improved by 39%. (SFv)

216 How has the average diet in developing countries improved in calories consumed per day from the years 1961 to 1989?

The number of calories per person per day has improved as follows:

Food supplies for direct human consumption

	1961-63	1969-71	1979-81	1987-89
World	2290	2430	2600	2700
Developing countries	1930	2100	2330	2470
Least-developed countries	1930	1980	2050	2050
Low income countries	1840	2010	2210	2380
(SF91p14)				

217 How many developing countries have improved their per caput food production during the years of record population growth since 1948-1952?

Substantially all developing countries have made substantial improvements in their per caput food production since 1948-1952. The average improvement has been about 39%. (SF 1953-1993)

218 What is the recommended number of calories which should be consumed each day?

Adjusted for size, sex, age, and activity level of each person, the recommended number of calories that should be consumed each day is about 2,200. People in colder climates need perhaps 10% more calories than people in warmer climates to make up for calories burned to maintain body temperature. Men usually need more calories than women because the average man is larger than the average woman. A man of the same weight as a woman usually needs more calories, in part because women are better insulated and in part because, on average, men are more muscular.

Children		Males		Females	
Age	Calories	Age	Calories	Age	Calories
0	800	11-14	2700	11-14	2200
1-3	1300	15-18	2800	15-22	2100
4-6	1700	19-22	2900	23-50	2000
7-10	2400	23-50	2700	51+	1800
		51+	2400		

(FN) (except children age 0 estimated by author)

The preceding data for various ages indicates that the average recommended calories for the total population is slightly less than 2,200 calories per day in developing countries.

219 In how many countries have people improved the average diet by increasing the number of calories consumed?

The average diet has improved in nearly all developing countries. In 1961-63, 74% of the people of developing countries lived in countries where the average diet was less than 2,000 calories. By 1987-89, this had been reduced to 6%. In 1987-1989, 50% of the population of developing countries lived in countries with an average diet of more than 2,600 calories, and 86% of the people in developing countries lived in countries with an average diet having more calories than the 2,200 daily calorie recommendation by the Food and Nutrition Board of the U.S. National Academy of Sciences-National Research Council (SF91 p 14, p 221)(FN).

Distribution of Developing Countries by Per Caput Food Supplies
kcal per caput/day

Year	under 2,000 number of countries	under 2,000 % of population	2,000-2,600 number of countries	2,000-2,600 % of population	over 2,600 number of countries	over 2,600 % of population	total population millions
1961-63	46	74	75	24	9	2	2130
1969-71	25	43	89	52	16	5	2601
1979-81	13	6	77	77	39	16	3252
1987-89	12	6	62	44	56	50	3845
(SF91 p 14)							

220 Has food production in the developing countries increased faster than population has grown?

Yes. Food production in developing countries increased more than 40% between 1947 and 1991.

221 How have cereal and meat production increased?

Cereal production comprises wheat, rice and similar grains. It is important as a measure of whether there is enough food production to keep everyone healthy and sufficiently fed. Meat production is not necessary to keep everyone healthy and sufficiently fed. Meat is a luxury food which is eaten by those who are wealthy enough to eat what they want. Meat production is a good measure of the distance above and beyond a healthy diet that a country's food production has progressed.

Volume of Production of Major Agricultural, Fishery and Forest Products

Year World (Millions of tons)	1981	1982	1983	1984	1985	1986	1987	1988	1989	1990	1991	annual rate of change % 1981-1990
Cereals	1646	1708	1640	1800	1839	1854	1788	1749	1885	1971	1887	1.45
Wheat	454	481	493	516	504	535	510	507	543	601	553	1.97
Rice, Paddy	412	425	451	468	471	471	464	491	516	522	518	2.26
Meat	138	139	143	147	152	157	162	169	171	176	179	2.87
(SF92 p197)												

	1948-52*	1960*	1970	1980	1990	% increase 1948-90	% increase 1970-90
Cereals	na	na	1215	1566	1971	na	62%
Wheat	155	221	318	446	601	288%	94%
Rice, Paddy	110	159	316	399	522	375%	65%
Meat	40	60	107	133	176	340%	64%
* Excluding Mainland China (SFv)							

222 What is the most common technique population control advocates use to mislead the public?

The most common technique population control advocates use to mislead the public is one of focusing attention on unusual or less important facts while ignoring the true overall situation. The following example, one among hundreds, of the use of this technique is analyzed in detail.

Population control advocate and former anti-Vietnam War activist Jane Fonda, speaking to the UN on September 20, 1993, focused on grain production to falsely claim the world was facing food shortages because of excess population growth. The real problem was just the opposite. There had been so much farm production that prices collapsed and governments had to step in to force farmers to grow less so that the massive supply of excess grain could be eaten and prices could rebound.

Fonda stated, "The production of grain, considered to (be) the most basic economic measure of human well being, increased 2.6 times from 1950 to 1984, much more than the population increased during the same time period, leading to an increase of grain consumption per capita of 40%. But in the nine years since 1984, grain output has only expanded 1% a year, falling behind population and leading to a per capita decline of 1% per year. According to Lester Brown . . . " (Fonda went on to cite Brown of Worldwatch Institute for the proposition that the whole world would soon be eating worse than the Chinese currently ate.)

The first step in Fonda's effort to mislead others into believing that the world was eating worse than before was to choose an unusual first year, 1984, thus distorting the comparison. Fonda talked as if 1984 was a typical year, but in actuality, 1984 was a year of atypically large grain production, which caused such a large surplus that governments had to take steps to cut food production. This made succeeding years appear poor by comparison. It was true that there was only a 5% increase in grain production between 1984 and 1991, but between 1983 and 1991, the increase in grain production was 15%, far greater than the corresponding increase in population and totally against the situation Fonda tried to represent.

Fonda's second step was to ignore facts indicating that the world was actually eating better. People who eat more meat are not starving. Instead, they are eating a more expensive diet. World meat production increased by 22% from 1984 to 1991.

Fonda also ignored data indicating that peoples' diets actually improved since 1984. Grain is only part of the food grown. Far from declining, per capita food production in developing countries actually improved 6% from 1984 to 1991.

Further, Fonda, in comparing 1984 to 1991, failed to mention the importance of temporary regional strife and the variations that occur over different areas. 1984 was a good year in the USSR and Eastern Europe, but 1991 was a year of revolution, which caused a grain production drop of 5% from 1984 levels. 1991 was also a year of low grain demand in North America and a year of low demand for North American grain exports. Even with the resulting 7% lower grain production than in 1984, North America still had plenty of grain. Africa and Asia were where food supply was most critical, and Africa increased its grain production by 47% between 1984 and 1991, while the developing countries of the Far East increased grain production by 12%. (SF92 pp 197-205)

The UNFAO points out the real reasons for the situation Fonda misleadingly described: "International market prices fell after 1981 . . . publicly held stocks. [of grain and other price-supported foods] rapidly increased. . . . These problems led to policy adjustments during the period 1981-1985. Supply controls were applied in the form of acreage reduction measures . . . Throughout the 1980s, a series of export promotion initiatives were taken . . . difficulties were the result of depressed agricultural exports, high interest rates, supply surpluses, increased farm programme costs and reduced market shares for US agricultural exports. . . . The main pressure for change in the CAP during the 1980s came through the problem of oversupply . . . As agricultural production increased and oversupply emerged . . . the problem of oversupply remains . . ."(SF91 pp 124, 125)

Fonda ignored the cause of the reduction in grain production as outlined above by the UNFAO. The multiplying of the amount of grain production by 2.6 during a time (1950-1984) when population did not even double severely depressed the price of grain, thereby removing incentives for farmers to grow more. During the 1950's and 1960's, a bushel of grain sold for about the same as a barrel of oil, but during the 1970's and 1980's, the price of grain decreased in real terms to about 20% of the 1950 price when allowance is made for inflation, to as low as about 10% of the price of a barrel of oil. Faced with massive grain surpluses, farmers of the developed nations reduced grain production after 1984. Farmers of the Near East and Africa, not faced with massive grain surpluses, increased grain production by more than 40% between 1984 and 1991. (SF92, pp 202, 204)

Thus, the true facts relating to grain production were the opposite of the impression Fonda tried to give in her speech. (FO)

223 How has production of grain, wheat, rice and meat increased in comparison with population?

Year World (million tons)	average 1948-52	1960	1970	1980	1990
Total cereals	na	na	1,215	1,566	1,952
Wheat	155	222	318	446	597
Rice	111	158	316	399	518
Total meat	40	60	107	133	175(SFv)
Population (millions)	2516	3020	3698	4448	5292

224 Why has food production increased faster than population has grown in recent years?

Experts compared how food was grown in high-yield production areas with how food was grown in low-yield production areas. High yield techniques used in low yield areas increased yield.

Technology continues to advance. Inexpensive techniques for making water wells permitted hundreds of thousands of tube wells to be drilled in India, thereby eliminating much of the problem caused by erratic rain. Fertilizer use was multiplied, eliminating low yields caused by marginal soils. Pesticides and better weather forecasting reduced causes of crop loss. Developing country farmers proved willing and able to learn and apply improved techniques. Better machinery and many additional improvements contributed to higher yields. Production has more than tripled since 1948 with little need for increased growing land. (SFv)

225 Why is food production likely to increase faster than population growth in the developing countries in the future?

Genetic engineering should vastly improve the effectiveness of seeds. Solar collectors should make inexpensive electricity available. Plant life grown from about .0002% of incoming sunlight is now consumed by people and their animals, leaving room for vast increases in efficiency. All of the techniques used to increase production since 1948 can be applied more effectively.

226 What has the UN said about how much of the world's arable land has been in use?

One-third of potential agricultural land has been used, dropping to one-sixth if forested land is included.

The following land data, taken from the *UN Statistical Yearbook*, 1970, pp 110-113, is still substantially correct.

2/3 OF LAND POTENTIALLY ARABLE

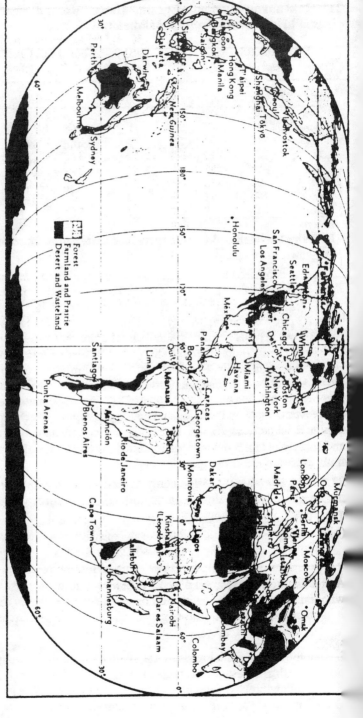

Forest
Farmland and Prairie
Desert and Wasteland

Place	Land Area 10,000 km²	Agricultural land (Potential)	Land Under Crops Total	% Total Land	% Ag & For Land	Forest Land	% Other Land Forest	Land
World	13,392	4407	1406	11%	17%	4068	30%	4917
Africa	3,030	1047	204	7	12	629	21	1354
N. Amer.	2,241	627	253	12	17	815	36	799
S. Amer.	1,784	497	89	5	7	927	52	360
Asia	2,753	893	444	16	31	565	21	1295
China	956	287	109	11	28	77	8	592
India	328	178	164	50	68	61	18	89
Indnsa	190	13	13	7	8	152	80	25
Japan	37	7	7	15	18	25	68	5
Europe	493	240	149	30	40	140	28	113
Netherlands	3.6	2.2	.91	25	36	0.3	8	1.1
UK	24.4	19.4	7.4	28	35	1.9	8	3.1

(SY70 pp 110-113)

England and the Netherlands are about 15 times as crowded as the USA and more than 10 times as crowded as the world. When we consider that they are getting along fine and are using less than 40 percent of their agricultural land, we see that those who have claimed the world might not be able to feed everyone are incorrect. India is using only two-thirds of its agricultural and forest land to grow crops and feeds its people more than the 2,200 calories per day recommended by the U.S. Japan uses 18 percent of its agricultural and forest land for crops and is troubled with vast surpluses and complaints from other countries like the U.S. that are prevented from exporting food to Japan.

227 How much potential agricultural land is there in the world?

Total Land Area (billion hectares)	Arable Land	Meadows & Pastureland	Forest	Desert & Unsuitable
13.6	1.43	2.58	4.10	5.42

Arable land can be increased to the following totals:

with existing methods and no capital	with capital investment	with new methods & capital investment
2.67	5.49	9.33

(MK)

228 People of how many of the most populated developing countries consume enough calories?

The most populated developing countries are: China, India, Indonesia, Brazil, Bangladesh, Pakistan, Nigeria, Mexico, Vietnam, Philippines, Turkey, Thailand and Iran. (Q520) In 1988-1990, the people of all these countries except Bangladesh, where the average daily intake was 2,037 calories, (SF92 pp 255-257) averaged at least the 2,200 calories per day recommended for a healthy diet. (FN)

229 How accurate are the assertions of Planned Parenthood about the world food situation?

In its first paragraph, a recent Planned Parenthood fund-raising letter claims: "Each day, 38,000 people perish for lack of food and water." This is false. (See Q 207)

230 How costly would it be to produce a machine that would prevent malnutrition?

The UNFAO claims that a machine costing $1,000 can convert plant matter such as leaves, clover, alfalfa, etc., into human food. The food can be used in drinks, cakes, biscuits, soups, stews, pasta, etc. Ten million dollars spent for 10,000 machines properly distributed might prevent most human malnutrition caused by a lack of food. (CE)

REFERENCES

(CE)   United Nations Food and Agricultural Organization magazine *Ceres*, Sept/Oct 1992, p 4
(FN)   Recommended daily allowances for calories for normally active persons in a temperate climate; source, Food & Nutrition Board, National Academy of Sciences-National Research Council; revised 1979-1980 as published under "Nutrition" in *World Book Encyclopedia*, 1986
(FO)   Jane Fonda, former anti-war activist and wife of Ted Turner, owner of CNN, gave a speech on Population to the UN on September 20, 1993, in which she omitted massive contradictory data and claimed that the fact that more grain per person was not being grown after 1984 meant that there were too many people and everyone could not be fed.
(MK)   K.M. Malin, *Food Resources of the Earth* Vol 3 p 6, Proceedings of the World Population Conference, UN 1967
(PB)   Paul Ehrlich, *Population Bomb*, 1968, 1970
(PE)   Paul Ehrlich and Anne Ehrlich, *Population Explosion*, (1990) Simon & Schuster, NY
(PR)   Paul Ehrlich, et al., *Population, Resources, Environment*, (1972)
(SF)   Food and Agriculture Organization of the United Nations, *The State of Food and Agriculture*, This is an annual report, so the year follows the (SF). The term "v" means various years can be compared to verify the reference.
(SW)   *The State of the World's Children 1993* (UNICEF, United Nations International Children's Emergency Fund), Oxford Press
(SY)   1970 UN *Statistical Yearbook*
(WD)   *World Development Report 1993* (World Bank) Oxford University Press
(WW)   Worldwatch Institute publishes reports at least annually. These reports typically focus in on some isolated non-typical area of non-improvement and allege that it is representative of the rest of the food situation, when, in fact, it is likely to be the worst news among generally good news.

CHAPTER 3

RESOURCES AND ENERGY

301 What do advocates of population control say about resources and energy?

302 What do opponents of population control say about resources and energy?

303 How can one determine if the advocates or opponents of
population control are correct?

304 Have the advocates and opponents of population control
ever made exactly contradictory predictions of the future, so
that we could see which prediction was more correct?

305 Why has the price of all mineral resources always declined
in real price over the long run?

306 What causes resources to increase and prices of resources
to decrease?

307 Can "known reserves" actually increase?

308 How large are world petroleum reserves?

309 Have U.S. petroleum reserves declined?

310 Why have U.S. petroleum reserves declined?

311 Can U.S. Government predictions of future petroleum supplies be trusted?

312 Why have U.S. Government estimates of future petroleum
supplies been so inaccurate?

313 How much potential petroleum is there in the world?

314 How are oil fields formed?

315 How big are large Middle East oil fields?

316 How do gasoline pump prices indicate if we are running
out of petroleum?

317 What was the cost of producing the petroleum we have been
using in recent years?

318 What does the cost of developing oil fields and the production cost tell us about future petroleum reserves?

319 How much of the earth's surface has been well explored
for petroleum?

320 Why is some petroleum less expensive to develop and produce?

321 How can I check supplies or see if the world or the U.S. is
running out of petroleum or any removable resource or mineral?

322 What were 1991 natural gas reserves?

323 What is the state of coal reserves?

324 What are other fuel reserves in addition to petroleum, natural gas and coal?

325 What are the major non-fuel sources of energy?

326 How effective is science in substituting one resource
for another?

327 What caused the revolutionary ability to bypass resource limitations?

328 What permits more value to be derived with fewer resources?

329 How much water is there in the world?

330 Is clean water becoming easier to obtain?

331 How many people lack clean water?

332 Are there places which no longer have sufficient water?

333 Why has desertification not caused more problems?

334 How can agricultural water be made more efficient?

335 Can vast amounts of non-agricultural water be saved?

336 How much solar energy does the earth receive?

337 How effective are we in tapping solar energy?

338 Is the world going to run low on oxygen?

339 Is the world going to run low on wood?

301 What do advocates of population control say about resources and energy?

Advocates of population control allege that we will soon run short of or out of certain important resources and energy, especially petroleum, unless we accept population control.

They claim that our supply of petroleum, natural gas, coal, metals and other removable resources is finite and so limited that the supply is in danger of exhaustion if depleted at current rates of use. They contend that the rate of depletion is proportional to the population and that limited resources will become costlier as they are depleted

Advocates of population control deny that advancing technology permits more efficient utilization of resources which prevents scarcity and keeps resource cost reasonable.

302 What do opponents of population control say about resources and energy?

Opponents of population control deny that serious permanent shortages of resources will occur. Rather they allege that all future resource scarcities will be caused by monopoly or government interference as opposed to depleted resources.

While opponents admit that the supply of non-renewable resource is finite, they allege that the supply is so large that resource exhaustion will not occur. They argue that the only meaningful resource question is the cost of resource production, and that, historically, as reserves are supplemented, resources have become more abundant with a subsequent reduction in their cost.

Opponents maintain that improved technology reduces the cost of producing resources faster than utilization increases prices, that the long resource price trend is downward for all resources. Advancing technology permits increased efficiency, so that more can be done with fewer resources.

Opponents claim that all previous predictions of resource scarcity by population control advocates have proven false, and that predictions by opponents that advancing technology would provide increasingly plentiful and less expensive resources have proven accurate.

303 How can one determine if the advocates or opponents of population control are correct?

If the advocates of population control are correct, we are about to run out of many important resources. If so, each of the following will be correct.

a) We should have run out of some resources.

b) Reserves of most resources should have decreased, both in terms of how long they will last and in terms of how much there is in reserve.

c) Prices of most minerals and energy should have substantially increased if we have come closer to running out.

d) It should be impossible to show that there are vast amounts of important resources yet to be removed from the earth or that reserves can increase.

e) Advancing technology has not substantially improved efficiency of resource use.

304 Have the advocates and opponents of population control ever made exactly contradictory predictions of the future, so that we could see which prediction was more correct?

Paul Ehrlich is the most famous advocate of population control and Julian Simon is the most famous opponent of population control. In 1981, they made a public bet. Ehrlich bet Simon that Ehrlich could predict five non-government-controlled resources that would increase in real price over the next ten years. Ehrlich selected five resources that he believed were the most likely to increase in price between 1981 and 1991. By 1991, Ehrlich was wrong in each case. The price of each of the five resources had declined, so Simon won the bet. The prices of the resources Ehrlich had been most certain would increase actually decreased by more than half, an average of 56.7%, so Ehrlich paid Simon $567.07. (IB)

305 Why has the price of all mineral resources always declined in real price over the long run?

The price of all mineral resources has always declined in real price (price adjusted for inflation) over the long run because the reserves of all mineral resources always increase over the long run and the real cost of producing (removing from the earth and processing) the mineral resources always declines over the long run.

306 What causes resources to increase and prices of resources to decrease?

As time goes on, the most accessible resources are produced and used. Since they were the most accessible, they were the least costly to produce. The total amount of each resource is sufficient to satisfy human needs for many millions of years, although we can only produce a tiny fraction economically with today's technology. Reserves are that part of all the resources that are the least costly to remove and that usually are to be removed next. Reserves comprise in all cases less than one-millionth of the total amount of the mineral resource, such as petroleum or iron, that is known to exist.

By the time the reserves are all or mostly removed, the next least expensive part of the mineral that was originally too expensive to be counted as among the reserves usually then becomes the least expensive to produce. In every case, during the time necessary to produce the former reserves, new discoveries are made. In addition, technology advances so that minerals that were formerly too expensive to be counted as reserves are now less expensive to remove than the former reserves had been.

A hypothetical example may help in understanding this process. Assume a certain amount of petroleum can be produced for $1.00 per unit. These are the reserves. The next cheapest petroleum can be produced for $1.05 per unit. These units were not initially counted among reserves because they cost 5% more per unit than the reserves. It takes many years to produce the reserves. During the time it takes to produce the reserves, improvements in production permit the formerly $1.05 per unit petroleum to be produced for 95 cents. In addition, new petroleum is discovered that can be produced for 95 cents per unit using the new technology. Even though the formerly cheapest petroleum that cost one dollar per unit has been produced and is no longer available, it has been replaced in the new reserves by other petroleum that now costs 95 cents per unit to produce. This process has been going on for some resources for thousands of years and there is no reason to doubt that it will continue. For detailed information relating to all major removable resources, see *Ultimate Resource* (1994) by Julian Simon.

307 Can "known reserves" actually increase?

If there is growing demand for resources, they usually increase over the short run and always increase over the long run. For a detailed analysis, refer to *Ultimate Resource* by Julian Simon.

Over relatively short periods of time of a few years, known reserves usually (but not always) increase. Over a long period of time all known reserves have increased. Based on this history and on the theory that explains it, opponents of population control allege that known reserves of all useful resources will always increase over long periods of time. The reader can verify that present reserves of the above minerals have increased at the time this book is read by checking reserves in the *US Minerals Yearbook* or the *UN Statistical Yearbook*.

308 How large are world petroleum reserves?

World petroleum reserves have been about one trillion barrels in the 1990's, gradually increasing from about 800 billion barrels in the 1980s. That is enough for about 40 years at present rates of use. Both the amount of petroleum in reserves and the number of years' production (reserves divided by amount produced each year) that the stated reserves would provide are at historical maximums. This indicates that recoverable supplies of petroleum are becoming more plentiful, not more scarce. (DE a) Petroleum reserves are defined by two magazines, *World Oil* and *Oil and Gas Journal*, then republished by the U.S. Department of Energy, which accepts their estimates. 1992 petroleum reserves are as follows: (EP)

Reserves billion barrels	Oil Used Per Year billion barrels	Years' Production in reserves	Source
967.1	24.163	40	*World Oil*
989.4	24.163	41	*Oil & Gas Journal*

309 Have U.S. petroleum reserves declined?

US Petroleum reserves peaked about 1970 and since have declined to about three-fourths of the 1970 peak (DE a).

310 Why have U.S. petroleum reserves declined?

With foreign petroleum relatively inexpensive, there has been little incentive to develop slightly more expensive U.S. petroleum. There is still plenty of U.S. petroleum if a need to drill in the U.S. arises again. For example, many coastal areas known to contain petroleum are off limits to drilling by law, as is a giant extension adjacent to the Prudhoe Bay petroleum field in Alaska. With the world petroleum price so low because of vast inexpensive foreign reserves, more expensive U.S. petroleum cannot compete and is not developed.

311 Can U.S. Government predictions of future petroleum supplies be trusted?

U.S. Government predictions since 1866 of future oil production and reserves are given in the following table below the year. You be the judge.

Date & US Production (billion barrels)	Prediction	Reality
1866 .005	Synthetics available if oil production should end (U.S. Revenue Commission)	In next 120 yrs., U.S. produced about 120 billion bbls. Synthetics still available, but natural petroleum less expensive
1885 .02	Little or no chance for oil in California (U.S. Geological Survey)	20 billion barrels produced since in California, 1000 times U.S. 1885 requirement
1891 .05	Little or no chance for oil in Kansas or Texas (U.S. Geological Survey)	Texas has produced more oil than any other state, about 1000 times U.S. 1891 requirement
1908 .18	Maximum future supply of 22.5 billion bbls. (Officials of U.S. Geological Survey)	More than that was produced in just California and Texas
1914 .27	Total future production only 5.7 billion bbls (Officials of U.S. Geological Survey)	More than 5.7 billion bbls. produced each 3 years recently and more than that still remains in reserves
1920 .45	U.S. needs foreign oil and synthetics: peak domestic production almost reached (Director of U.S. Geological Survey)	.45 billion barrels, entire production that was supposed to be the most the U.S. could produce in a year has been about 15% of later annual U.S. production.
1931 .85	Must import as much foreign oil as possible to save domestic supply (Secretary of Interior)	During next 8 years imports discouraged and 14 billion bbls. found in the U.S. (about twice as much as was used)
1939	U.S. oil supplies will last only 13 years (radio broadcasts by Interior Department)	New reserves proven in one subsequent year were about equal to all U.S. reserves in 1939
1947 1.9	Sufficient oil cannot be found in U.S. (Chief of Petroleum Division)	The next year, more U.S. oil was found than in any previous year

(Continued)

Date & U.S. Production (billion barrels)	Prediction	Reality
1949 2.0	End of U.S. oil supply almost in sight (Secretary of Interior)	Oil found next 40 years was 4 times as much as found in all history before 1950
1973 3.5	U.S. Geological Survey estimated that 270,000 million tons of oil, about 5.4 trillion bbls., would eventually be found in U.S.	This estimate, more than all oil found in entire world, was made as OPEC raised prices and may be a lie made in hope of holding price down. U.S. reserves have since declined.

312 Why have U.S. Government estimates of future petroleum supplies been so inaccurate?

When the issue relates to politics or big money, those having an opportunity frequently attempt to influence decisions by lying.

313 How much potential petroleum is there in the world?

Petroleum is a combination of carbon, hydrogen, and various impurities. There are several billion billion tons of carbon in the earth's lithosphere, which could provide nearly a billion years' worth of petroleum at present rates of use. Because carbon and hydrogen are light elements, most of this potential petroleum is probably relatively close to the surface of the earth. Unfortunately, all but a tiny part of this potential petroleum is so thinly spread out that it will probably never be recovered.

314 How are oil fields formed?

The formation of a commercially valuable oil or natural gas reservoir depends on formations that concentrate the petroleum. First there must be underlying rocks that provide a source of organic material. Since carbon and hydrogen are very light, there is a tendency for them to be forced upward. Secondly, there must be a geological structure that will halt the upward migration of the hydrocarbons, such as a layer of salt, some impervious rock or even a geological fault.

The most valuable oil reservoirs are structures in which the rocks are porous, enabling them to contain large quantities of oil or gas (up to 30% by volume), and also thick, so that a hole drilled in the ground can collect hydrocarbons rapidly.

315 How big are large Middle East oil fields?

The Burgan field in Kuwait is an underground layer of sandstone 1,300 feet thick, conservatively estimated to have contained 10 billion tons of recoverable crude. The Ghawar field in Saudi Arabia, an elliptical geological structure 135 miles long, consists of four layers of limestone separated from each other and capped on top by layers of salt. It has been estimated to contain more than 6 billion tons of petroleum. Both countries have other fields.

316 How do gasoline pump prices indicate if we are running out of petroleum?

To easily check the petroleum supply, look at the price charged for gasoline. In 1981, unleaded regular averaged $1.38 per gallon. Since then the value of the dollar has been reduced substantially by inflation, so in constant value dollars, gasoline should now cost about $2.00 per gallon. If we were running out of petroleum, the price would have increased to far more than $3.00 per gallon as predicted by the U.S. Government *Global 2000* report in 1980. Compare $3.00 per gallon to the price you pay. (DEm)

317 What was the cost of producing the petroleum we have been using in recent years?

In the Middle East, the capital cost of development, including roads, pipelines, harbors, equipment and drilling costs, etc., has been less than 10 cents per barrel, which is less than one quarter of a penny per gallon. In countries such as Libya or Indonesia, the cost has been about twice as much, about half a penny per gallon. In Venezuela, the cost has been slightly less than a penny per gallon. In the U.S., if one did not count all the tax benefits, the cost of developing petroleum has averaged about three cents per gallon. In the North Sea, development costs averaged about five cents per gallon and in Alaska, slightly more. The cost of producing the petroleum is about equal to the cost of developing the petroleum. These costs do not include royalties paid to the owner of the mineral rights, transportation, refining and distribution costs. More recently developed petroleum and petroleum developed in the future are likely to be more expensive, but still cheap enough to indicate that there is a great deal of petroleum yet to be added to reserves.

318 What does the cost of developing oil fields and the production cost tell us about future petroleum reserves?

If they are still producing petroleum from fields where the cost is less than a penny per gallon, we are not about to run low on petroleum.

319 How much of the earth's surface has been well explored for petroleum?

When you look at a petroleum industry map of oil fields (PE), it appears that less than 10% of the earth's land surface has been well explored for oil fields. According to the most popular theory, oil has been formed from the remains of tiny marine plants and animals. If so, substantially all the petroleum should be in the ocean which is largely unexplored. Most encyclopedias have a petroleum production area map. (WB)

320 Why is some petroleum less expensive to develop and produce?

Larger oil fields can both be found and worked most cheaply. The costs of exploration, discovery (test drilling) and development are spread over a larger quantity of oil or natural gas. Another factor is the rate at which a well yields oil or natural gas. Many Saudi Arabian oil wells have averaged 7,000 barrels of oil a day, whereas in the US a typical capacity is 50 to 100 barrels a day. This is why the US cost is higher.

321 How can I check supplies or see if the world or the U.S. is running out of petroleum or any removable resource or mineral?

Most large libraries have appropriate reference material, such as *Minerals Yearbook* published annually by the U.S. Department of the Interior, annual or monthly *Energy Review* by the Department of Energy or an appropriate UN publication such as the *UN Statistical Yearbook*. For petroleum or natural gas, check the magazines *World Oil* or *Oil and Gas Journal*, which are relied on by the U.S. Energy Department.

322 What were 1991 natural gas reserves?

In 1991, natural gas reserves were listed as about 4,211 trillion cubic feet by *Oil and Gas Journal* and 4,326 trillion cubic feet by *World Oil* (DE a)(EP). World use is 73 trillion cubic feet per year, so natural gas reserves are sufficient for nearly 60 years at present rates of use. The same analysis previously made of petroleum reserves applies to natural gas reserves. They are growing and there is every reason to expect additional growth of natural gas reserves in the future.

323 What is the state of coal reserves?

Both the world and the U.S. have enormous coal reserves sufficient for hundreds of years of production. (MY)

324 What are other fuel reserves in addition to petroleum, natural gas and coal?

When carbon/hydrogen fuel is thin enough and concentrated enough to flow easily so that we can remove it easily, we call it petroleum. When it is too thick to flow or not concentrated enough, we call it tar sands or oil shale. Tar sands and oil shale can be removed, but at a higher cost than petroleum. They are nevertheless important. If there were no tar sands and oil shale, OPEC would probably raise the price of oil. OPEC leaders have made no secret of their intention to keep the price of petroleum as high as possible, with the ceiling being just under the price of tar sands, oil shale and other competing energy sources for petroleum needs such as coal gasification. There are what amount to more dilute forms of coal, such as peat, which are used in some countries without massive coal deposits.

325 What are the major non-fuel sources of energy?

Fuel provides about 95% of energy. Water power provides about 2%. Other sources are tidal and wind power which provide some power, but only at carefully selected locations with optimum conditions. Wind power could provide substantial additional power, but tidal power appears to be very limited in potential. Conversion of solar energy to electricity does not furnish much power now, but is projected to produce enormous amounts of energy before the year 2000. (EC)

326 How effective is science in substituting one resource for another?

U Thant, Secretary General of the UN, stated: "The central stupendous truth about developed economies today is that they can have—in anything but the shortest run—the kind and scale of resources they decide to have . . . It is no longer resources that limit decisions. It is the decision that makes the resources. This is the fundamental revolutionary change—perhaps the most revolutionary man has ever known." (SC)

327 What caused the revolutionary ability to bypass resource limitations?

During the Cold War, certain nations saw that certain strategic materials might be cut off. To prevent serious shortages, they developed new materials technologies, which together with information and biotechnology constitute the basis of the new industrial revolution. (MM 4)

328 What permits more value to be derived with fewer resources?

a) "Once the process of initial industrialization is complete, heavy infrastructures are in place; they include roads, railways, buildings, pipelines, basic installations for the heavy industry, all of which had involved large investments in materials (steel, non-ferrous metals, concrete, glass, plastics, etc.). The basic needs of the population in terms of durable goods are also substantially satisfied.

34

The need for resources thus is limited mostly to repair, replacement and improvement."

b) "Technology makes greater useful output possible with fewer resources. For example, a cable was laid across the Atlantic Ocean to permit communication. Massive structures were built to permit national TV. With satellites, the cable and structures are no longer necessary, since a signal can be transmitted up to a satellite, then down to nearly half the world.

"The weight of an average auto declined by more than 15% from 1976 to 1987, although performance and safety improved. The weight to power ratio of a locomotive has decreased by about a factor of 100 from 1850 to now. In some cases, technological advances have brought a completely new approach to the same problem." (MM 5)

329 How much water is there in the world?

There are 278.11 kilograms of sea water per square centimeter of the earth's surface. The weight of the water is $14,060 \times 10^{20}$ grams. The volume of the water is 1.370 billion cubic kilometers. Ninety-eight percent of the water is salty and in the ocean. Ninety-eight percent of the fresh water is in ice, nearly all of it in Antarctica. This amounts to 280×10^{20} grams of ice. The fresh water amounts to 5×10^{20} grams. This amounts to nearly 100 billion grams of fresh water for every person on earth. In the atmosphere there is 5×10^{18} grams of water. This amounts to nearly 10 million pounds of water in the atmosphere for every person on earth. Translating into pounds, that means nearly a billion pounds of fresh water for each person on earth, or 16 thousand trillion cubic feet of fresh water, or enough to cover the entire surface of the earth more than 3 feet deep, or enough to cover all the land surface of the earth more than 13 feet deep, and that is without desalting any of the salt water in the ocean. With this vast amount of water existing in freshwater lakes, rivers, etc., it is obvious that the only problem with water is cleanliness in certain areas, and certain areas that do not have a reasonable share of the water. There is enough fresh water in the north and south polar ice caps to cover the entire land surface of the earth with ice approximately 600 feet thick. This ice is equal to 1,000 years' flow of all rivers and about equal to 200 years' rainfall. There are lakes in the world, such as Superior or Baikal, which each contain more than enough water to cover all the land in the world several inches deep. (WN) One trillion tons of sea water are evaporated each day (NG) by the trillion horsepower constantly received from the sun, and it falls back as rain, snow or sleet. Each day about 50,000 storms each release about one megaton of energy. (NG)

330 Is clean water becoming easier to obtain?

Yes, population growth permits the cost of providing clean water to be spread over more people so the cost per person decreases.

". . . the lack of adequate nutrition, safe water supply, and basic education—are also now becoming susceptible to a combination of new technologies, falling costs, and community-based strategies. The cost of providing clean water in Africa, for example, has been halved since the 1980s and now stands at an average figure of about $20 per person per year." (SW6)

331 How many people lack clean water?

In the least developed countries, having 519 million people, 47% have clean water, 61% of urban, and 42% of rural inhabitants. In the developing countries, having 4,147 million people, 72% have clean water, 84% of urban and 65% of rural inhabitants. These percentages having clean water have substantially increased in recent years as population has grown. In 95% of the countries having about 97% of the population, urban areas are more likely to have safe water. More populous and more crowded countries are more likely to have safe water. (SW69, 73)

332 Are there places which no longer have sufficient water?

Rainfall varies. Where rainfall is marginal for the agriculture, in dry years, crop production will be reduced. Poor farming techniques can cause desertification, which is the turning of formerly marginal farming land into desert or sub-marginal farming land. Of course, this process can be reversed by planting trees and other techniques. Nevertheless, in areas of severe desertification, less food will be grown, so either the people will have to move out, or they will have to bring food in.

333 Why has desertification not caused more problems?

The increase in carbon dioxide in the atmosphere is helping plants make do with far less water, so desertification has had less effect than many initially feared. Food production and per capita food production are increasing even in most countries suffering from some desertification. Increased carbon dioxide enables plants to breathe in the carbon dioxide they need more quickly, so they lose less water, and consequently can get by with less water. Modern techniques can grow crops with less than 10% of the water formerly considered necessary.

334 How can agricultural water be made more efficient?

Two-thirds of removed water is used for irrigation. Irrigation is estimated to be less than 40% efficient in water use. Trenches and spraying in the air are inefficient. Changing continuous stream irrigation to surge irrigation reduces water use 15-50%. A new sprinkler design, low energy precision application is about 95% efficient. Monitoring soil moisture to reduce unneeded irrigation such as by gypsum blocks reduces water use by nearly 50%. Drip irrigation reduces salinization and often achieves efficiencies of 95%

Maintaining present systems and cutting losses from present systems, such as by paving canals to reduce loss, is cost-efficient. Proper pricing reduces water use. Smaller-scale projects, such as tube wells, rather than large dams, are frequently more efficient. Terracing and proper contouring save water. Various dry farming techniques can be adapted to most of the world's dry agriculture. (L099-135) In nearly all areas where agriculture is threatened by lack of water, proper techniques can solve foreseeable water shortages. Providing means to obtain fertilizer is usually very cost efficient. While there is a cost for some of these techniques or for necessary material or machinery, the cost is far less than the cost of shipping in food to prevent periodic food shortages, or the cost of displaced refugees.

335 Can vast amounts of non-agricultural water be saved?

Underpricing water leads to vast waste. It prevents water-saving techniques from being cost-effective. Industrial water recycling vastly reduces water use and sewage problems. At least fourfold increases in industrial water efficiency are possible. Less water can be used for certain purposes, such as toilet flushing. Making people water-saving conscious reduces water use. Homes can recycle. For example, shower water can be reused in toilets or washing machines. Proper design and maintenance reduces waste in the water distribution system. (L0136-182) While rainfall will vary and shortages will occur, we have the means to reduce water use where necessary to prevent nearly all the harm that might be caused by severe water shortages in the foreseeable future.

336 How much solar energy does the earth receive?

The earth receives 174 thousand trillion watts. This is more than 10,000 times as much energy as humans use. About 30% is directly reflected back into space as short-wave visible radiation, which makes the earth shine like the other planets. About 47% is converted to heat and transmitted back into space as long-wave radiation. About 23% evaporates water, which then rains and snows back on the earth. About 0.2% produces the wind, waves and currents. About .02%, which is about six times as much as man used in 1970, is used by plants to grow plant materials. Plant life grown from about .0002% of incoming sunlight is eaten by people or their animals.

337 How effective are we in tapping solar energy?

As this book is written, direct conversion of solar energy provides only a small proportion of total energy needs, but it looks like solar energy will soon substantially increase in importance.

Solar energy is primarily useful for minor energy needs such as space heating, water heating, electricity and cooking in isolated areas. A solar oven is having much good impact in developing nations, particularly in those areas where wood is scarce. Proper house design now makes solar space heating cost-effective. Solar water heaters are cost-effective only in areas with substantially above-average amounts of sunshine.

The direct conversion of sunshine to electricity was cost-effective twenty years ago only in the most isolated areas, such as on spacecraft. With time, the price of solar-electricity converters has come down from about 100 times as expensive to about twice as expensive as compared with most other sources of electricity. For example, solar collectors are the the most cost-effective way to generate electricity in isolated villages in developing countries where about a billion people live without electricity. Bringing electricity to these villages will cause a substantial improvement in quality of life.

If this downward trend in the cost of solar collectors continues, in a short time they will make a massive contribution to energy needs without pollution or extraction problems. Solar-generated electricity will supply a substantial part of the world's energy needs and will furnish price competition for petroleum, which will limit and perhaps reduce the top price for petroleum.

An alternative method of generating electricity from sunlight is the use of mirrors to focus sunlight on a container of special salts which store the heat from the sunlight for use in generating electricity. (EC)

338 Is the world going to run low on oxygen?

No. There is more oxygen on earth than any other element. On June 24, 1970, scientists of the Environmental Science Service Administration and the National Science Foundation issued a report on a three-year study into the composition of air at 78 sites around the world. Their finding: the amount of oxygen in the air in 1970 was precisely the same as the amount of oxygen in 1910.

The oxygen content of the air was 20.946% by volume in 1910, when it was analyzed by scientists of that period, and according to the 1967-1970 study, it is still 20.946% by volume.

In their commentary on the latest research, Dr. Lester Machta of the Environmental Science Services Administration and Ernest Hughes of the National Bureau of Standards declared that not only is oxygen just as plentiful as it ever was, but that "man's burning of coal, oil and gas would not have any appreciable effect on world oxygen supply even if all the known reserves of these fuels were to be consumed." There are approximately 10,000,000,000,000,000 tons of free oxygen in the atmosphere.

339 Is the world going to run low on wood?

No, but some areas will. In some parts of developing countries, people have removed too many trees without replanting and in some areas there has been desertification. There has been some reduction in tropical forest area.

Tropical forests cover such a vast percentage of the area of some countries such as Brazil that Brazilians might well ask why they have to maintain a higher percentage of their country in forest than their critics maintain in the critics' countries. (Please see Chapter 6, Species.) Overall, about one-third of earth's surface is forest. Forests in temperate areas are increasing. (SYv)

In the U.S., there are about 800 trees for every human. Timber prices are increasing not because of a lack of trees that could be cut, but because environmental limitations limit the potential cutting.

The increase in atmospheric CO_2 has apparently vastly increased the growth of trees, especially young trees. (ID)

REFERENCES

(CI)   Council on International Economic Policy, Executive Office of the President, Special Report, *Critical Imported Materials*, Washington DC (1974)

(DE a) annual energy review 1991, Energy Information Administration, U.S. Dept. of Energy

(DE m) ibid. monthly, March 1992

(EC)   Southern California Edison Co. press releases, October, 1993. *Time* magazine (Oct 18, 1993) published an article "Here Comes the Sun" by John Greenwald, relating to Edison research and a joint venture with Texas Instruments.

(EP)   1992 reserves were obtained by telephoning the Department of Energy. The reader can call the Department of Energy directly or can call his Congressman's office to verify energy information in this book or to obtain more current information

(IB)   *Investor's Business Daily* Jan 31, 1992, p 1

(ID)   *Carbon Dioxide and Global Change*, Sherwood Idso, IBR Press

(LO)   Sandra Postel, *Last Oasis* (1992) WW Norton & Co., NY, London

(MM)   *Materials and Mineral Resources*, talk given by Ugo Farinelli, ENEA, Rome, Italy, Nov 1991 at Pontifical Academy of Sciences study week on "Resources and Population," to be published

(MY)   *US Minerals Yearbook* published annually by U.S. Government

(NG)   *National Geographic*, 4/72, p 528

(PE)   *International Petroleum Encyclopedia* (1979), Petroleum Publishing Co.

(SC)   quoted in *The Secular City* by H. Cox, Macmillan, NY, p 184 (1965)

(SW)   *The State of the World's Children 1993* published for UNICEF by Oxford University Press, citing *Rural Water and Health: The Challenge to Water and Sanitation Professional, Waterfront* No 1, p 3, Feb1992, UNICEF, NY

(SYv)   *UN Statistical Yearbook*, various editions

(WB)   *World Book Encyclopedia* (1986), World Book, Inc., Chicago

(WN)   *World News of the Week*, Nov 15, 1971

CHAPTER 4

EARTH, EMPTY OR CROWDED?

401 What do advocates of population control say about available space?

402 What do opponents of population control say about available space?

403 How can we determine whether advocates or opponents of population control are correct about available space?

404 Isn't it true that the earth is a spaceship of limited size?

405 Is the earth running out of unused living space?

406 What are the weight, volume, area and land area of the world?

407 How much space do all the people take?

408 If the earth were reduced to the size of a house and people were reduced proportionately, what volume could contain all people?

409 How big an area would be required for all the world's people to stand, lie down, or have a big card game?

410 What is the total weight of all the people in the world?

411 What percent of the U.S. is covered by roads, sidewalks, parking lots, or other forms of paving?

412 What percentage of the U.S. is devoted to such uses as development, farming and forest?

413 How much of the world's surface and the surface of individual areas is taken up by housing?

414 How much of the world's surface is taken up by all buildings, roads, fences, and structures?

415 How much of the world's surface is taken by humanity's farms, roads, cities, etc?

416 If everyone in the world lived in the U.S. could they live better than they do now?

417 Is there actually more available space in the U.S. today than in prior years?

418 How big are the continents?

419 If everybody in the world lived in the U.S., how crowded would it be?

420 How crowded would it be if everyone lived in U.S. government-owned forests?

401 What do advocates of population control say about available space?

Advocates of population control allege that the earth only has so much space, and that as population increases, the average amount of space available for each person must decrease. They claim that many areas are too crowded already and say that additional people will make the earth too crowded.

402 What do opponents of population control say about available space?

Opponents of population control admit that the earth only has so much space and that as population increases, the average amount of space per person must decrease. They allege crowding is not a problem, because the earth is very large and little used. They claim that crowding is not caused by a lack of space, but rather by people moving to cities to pursue the higher quality of life available in more densely populated areas. They say almost all increase in population is or soon will be in cities, and anyone wishing to live in an uncrowded area has, and in the future will have, about as many choices as in the past.

403 How can we determine whether advocates or opponents of population control are correct about available space?

We can determine whether advocates or opponents of population control are correct about available space by determining how much space is available, how it is used, and whether there will be sufficient space for reasonable uses in the future. We should determine the following:

a) the percentage of the earth needed for farms, roads, buildings, and other required and desired uses;

b) how much space urbanization and the increase in the size of cities requires;

c) how much land is available and what type of land it is; and

d) how crowded the world is in readily understandable terms.

404 Isn't it true that the earth is a spaceship of limited size?

That is a cute metaphor which may be technically correct, but it is very deceiving unless one is capable of imagining a tremendously big space ship which is extremely empty and woefully undermanned.

405 Is the earth running out of unused living space?

Many Americans live in cities and assume the whole U.S. and the whole world are like their cities, but cities cover less than 1% of the earth's land surface. If you look at a population density map, you find that most square miles of land in the world have less than one family living in them. A kilometer is about five-eighths of a mile. If you divide the land of the earth into square kilometers, about half have nobody living in them. While large numbers of people believe some land is more desirable than other land, experience shows that people differ. Millions want to and do live in desert, mountain, cold, jungle or other areas that some might consider unlivable.

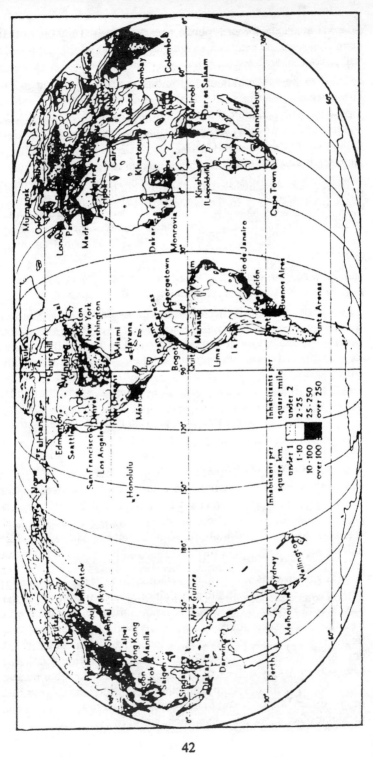

42

406 What are the weight, volume, area and land area of the world?

The total area of the world is about 197 million square miles (about 500 million square kilometers). The land area is about 58 million square miles (about 150 million square kilometers). The world weighs 6.5 times 10^{21} tons. If you wrote it out, you would first write a 65 and then 20 zeroes followed by the word "tons." The volume of the world is about 260 billion cubic miles (about 1065 billion cubic kilometers). (ME)

407 How much volume do all the people occupy?

If everyone were huddled together in a big ball, one person could walk from the center to the farthest person in about five minutes. (Calculation follows.)

There are about 6 billion people. Because children are lighter, people average in weight about 100 pounds each. Together, all people weigh about 100 pounds times six billion people or 600 billion pounds or 300 million tons.

People have a density similar to water or about 63 pounds per square foot. At about 100 pounds each, the world's people have a volume averaging 1.6 cubic feet per person. The volume of all people together is about six billion times 1.6 or about ten billion cubic feet. Volume of a sphere is 4/3 x pi x r x r x r. Cancel the 3 and the pi which are about equal. If the radius of the sphere is one-fourth mile or 1320 feet, volume equals about 4 x 1320 x 1320 x 1320 = more than 9 billion cubic feet, enough to pack in everyone. (Remember the earth is 260 billion cubic miles.)

A person can walk 440 yards, the radius of such a sphere, in about five minutes.

Many of the world's great cities have buildings big enough in volume to contain the entire world population. (Calculation of one city example: people weigh about 100 pounds and thus occupy less than 2 cubic feet, so 6 billion people occupy 10 billion cubic feet. Ceilings average 8 feet high, so 10 billion cubic feet require 1.25 billion square feet of floor inside buildings. New York is 763 square miles times 27.9 million square feet per square mile or 21 billion square feet. Buildings occupy more than 10% of New York's 21 billion square feet or more than the required 1.5 billion square feet, so you could fit everyone in only the first story of New York's buildings with the upper stories empty. Since New York has many tall buildings, it probably has many times the required 1.25 billion square feet inside buildings, and so do many other cities.) Hills more than 1,000 feet high (300 m) are bigger than all the people in the world would be if they were put in one place. If the area on which the Pentagon is built, including lawns (238 acres) held a building 900 feet high (some buildings are higher), you could put in it everyone in the world. (43,560 square feet per acre times 238 acres = area of more than 10 million square feet times 900 = 9 billion cubic feet.)

408 If the earth were reduced to the size of a house and people were reduced proportionately, what volume could contain all people?

Far less than one one-billionth of a cubic inch.

409 How big an area would be required for all the world's people to stand, lie down, or have a big card game?

All the people in the world could stand in about 143 square miles. In other words, if you had everybody in the world standing in one place, you could put them in about 20% of the area of Jacksonville, Florida, or 10% of the area of Juneau, Alaska, and have room left over. If everybody in the world wanted to lie down on one flat surface with nobody touching anybody else, you could put them all in about 650 square miles. In other words you could put all of them inside the city limits of Jacksonville or in any one of several other cities with room left over.

The calculation is: 6 billion people x 3 square feet per person lying on their sides equals 18 billion square feet divided by 27.9 million square feet per mile equals 650 square miles.

Since the earth's surface area is almost 200 million square miles, all the people could stand in less than one/one-millionth of the surface area of the world or about 143 square miles (less than 12 miles by 12 miles) as shown by the following calculation.

Since more than 20% of people are children, people's feet average about 8 inches by three inches or 24 square inches. People have two feet, so the total area of the average person's feet is about 48 square inches. One square foot is 144 square inches, so the feet of three people require one square foot of area, but let's double the required foot space to leave room for shoulders and assume 1.5 people per square foot. 6 billion divided by 1.5 = 4 billion square feet. There are almost 28 million square feet in a square mile, so 4 billion square feet divided by the number of square feet in a square mile, 27.9 million, is 143 square miles.

410 What is the total weight of all the people in the world?

There are about 6 billion people in the world averaging in weight about 100 pounds each, so that all together, they weigh about 300 million tons. This is about the weight of the bugs eaten by the world's spiders each month. This surprising statement is extrapolated from data by Dr. John A.L. Cooke, the American Museum of Natural History spider expert who has calculated the weight of insects eaten by spiders in certain areas of the world. (Please remember that when you see somebody step on a spider.) Also, each month the cattle of the world eat food weighing more than the world's people.

411 What percent of the U.S. is covered by roads, sidewalks, parking lots, or other forms of paving?

About one percent. The U.S. has about 4 million miles of road, more than 80% in rural areas. (CI)

The area of the US is about 3,600,000 square miles, so 1% of US area is about 36,000 square miles or 90,000 square kilometers. If you assume roads average 30 feet wide, all the roads take up less than 23,000 square miles, far less than one percent of U.S. area. The 30-foot-wide average is reasonable. Superhighways may average about 100 feet wide, but there are less than 100,000 miles of them. More than 80% of the total mileage is in rural areas and averages about 20 feet wide. Since 80% of mileage is rural, very little of which has adjacent parking or sidewalks, you can allot generous portions of area for all municipal paving and the relatively small amount of extra paving for parking lots, etc., in the U.S., and find all of the paving in the U.S. takes about 1% of total U.S. area. (This includes the space taken by unpaved roads but excludes unpaved areas in towns.) (CI) for road mileage.

412 What percentage of the U.S. is devoted to such uses as development, farming and forest?

About 3% of the U.S. is developed, including rural transportation areas. Note that most area defined as developed is not paved, so that the developed area (3%) is substantially higher than the paved area (1%) in Q411. 19% of the U.S. is crop land, which is about 30% of non-Federal land in the lower 48 states. More than 45% is forest, which is about 27% of non-Federal land in the lower 48 states. Other percentages are pasture 6% and 9%; range land 18% and 27%. (SA) (LU)

413 How much of the world's surface and the surface of individual areas is taken up by housing?

About 13,000 square miles. This is the author's estimate and is less than one-four-thousandth of the land surface area in the world. The following estimate is derived from housing data in the 1970 *UN Statistical Yearbook* and was updated by using data in *UN Compendium of Social Statistics & Indicators*, 1988. Numbers are rounded off. Assumptions include: 1) nations not giving data have area comparable to similar nations and 2) average size of a room is a function of the average income of the country.

Table 4-1

Place	Land Area (million sq. mile)	Millions of Rooms	Avg. Area (square feet)	Room Area (sq. mi.)	Fraction Area in Homes
World	58	3800	96	13,000	1/4000
Africa	12	400	75	1,400	1/8000
Asia	10.5	1500	80	4,300	1/2400
Europe	2	650	110	2,500	1/800
N Amer	8	460	140	2,300	1/3500
Lat Amer	8	300	100	1,100	1/7000
China	3.6	500	80	1,400	1/2500
India	1.2	400	75	1,100	1/1300
USSR	8.5	250	100	900	1/9000

414 How much of the world's surface is taken up by all buildings, roads, fences, and structures?

All the roads in the U.S. occupy 23,000 square miles (Q411). U.S. road mileage is 6.4 million km or about 4 million miles. The numbers for kilometers of roads in some other nations are as follows in millions of kilometers: Australia 0.8, Brazil 1.4, China 1.0, France 0.6, Germany 0.6, Indonesia 0.1, Iran 0.1, Italy 0.3, Japan 1.1, Mexico 0.2, Russia 0.9. From this it seems reasonable to assume that the world has less than 20 million kilometers (12.5 million miles) of roads averaging slightly more than 20 feet wide (foreign roads are narrower than U.S. roads) for a total area of about 50,000 square miles (130,000 sq km). Mileage of railroads is only a tiny fraction of road mileage. (CI)

If you add to the above total a generous allotment for all the fences, railroads, high power lines, etc., and assume that the area taken up by all these slightly exceeds the total area taken up by homes, you get approximately 65,000 square miles. Add all the homes and you get approximately 80,000 square miles.

In the U.S., the *US Statistical Abstract* indicates that homes take up 60% of all space constructed. Homes occupy an even greater percentage of total building area in the rest of the world. Accordingly, it is reasonable to presume that all the buildings other than homes take up about 10,000 square miles. This means when we add together all of man's artifacts such as homes, paving, buildings, etc., they take up about 90,000 square miles. This is one-sixth of 1% of the land area of the world of about 58 million square miles, and less than one-two-thousandth of the world total area of about 200 million square miles.

46

415 How much of the world's surface is taken by humanity's farms, roads, cities, etc?

Total farmland was estimated in 1967 to be far less than 1.5 billion hectares or far less than 6 million square miles. There has been little increase since. In the average year, most of this land is not harvested, but even if you assume it all is farmed, and add to it the 85,000 square miles for non-farm uses, you find people use about 3% of the earth's surface or 10% of the earth's land surface. (MK)

416 If everyone in the world lived in the U.S. could they live better than they do now?

Yes. They could have roomier residences with more space than they have now in an area less than the size of Alaska. If you include space for industry, parks, etc., and assume they live as urbanized as one-third of American people live, everybody in the world could have their homes, parks, etc., on about 15 percent of the U.S. land. The rest of the U.S. land would be sufficient to grow enough food to feed everybody in the world comparable to how they eat now, assuming yields comparable to those in the highest agricultural yield nations. Note that all the homes, roads, farms, etc., in the world now take up about twice the area of the U.S.

If everyone lived like they do in New York City (26,000/sq. mi.), they could all live in Arizona and New Mexico. (six billion divided by 26,000=230,000 square miles.) Each of 44 U.S. states alone could hold all the world's people if they were as densely populated as Manhattan in 1970. (687,802/sq mi, 6 billion divided by 687,802 = 8734 square miles, which is less than the area of each of 44 U.S. states, including small states such as Vermont, New Hampshire and Maryland.)

417 Is there actually more available space in the U.S. today than in previous years?

Yes. Urbanization takes less than 3% of U.S. land. This is calculated by assuming an urban population density comparable to that of the least densely populated large cities. Assume a population of 250,000,000, and a population density of 2,500 per square mile. Urban areas would be 1/2,500 of 250,000,000, or 100,000 square miles, less than 3% of the total U.S. area of about 3.6 million square miles, less than the area taken out of agriculture since 1945. (LU)

418 How big are the continents?

The earth land surface area is about 58 million square miles (about 150 million km²), of which 11.7 million (more than 30 million km²) is in Africa, 9.4 million (24.3 million km²) is in North America, about 7 million (18 million km²) is in South America, almost 17 million (almost 44 million km²) is in Asia, almost 3 million (7.7 million km²) is in Australia and the surrounding islands, and about

4 million (10.5 million km²) is in Europe. Seven million square miles are polar, of which 5.1 million (13.2 million km²) is in Antarctica, and almost 2 million square miles of polar area (about 5 million km²) is on other continents or polar islands. (DI)

419 If everybody in the world lived in the U.S., how crowded would it be?

If you've ever been to New Jersey, you've almost seen it. New Jersey in 1990 had a population density of more than 1,000 persons per square mile. The U.S. has an area of about 3.6 million square miles. Almost 6 billion people living in the U.S. would be a population density of about 1,600 people per square mile, or about 50% more crowded than New Jersey.

420 How crowded would it be if everyone lived in U.S. government-owned forests?

They would have more than twice the space the average U.S. family now has. The average U.S. family lives on less than a 7,000-square-foot lot, or less than one-sixth acre. U.S. government-owned forests comprise about 500 million acres, about 800,000 square miles, nearly 10 acres for every family in the country, about 400 times the area taken up by all the homes or 200 times the area taken up by all the buildings including homes. If every family in the world was put in U.S. federal forests, each family would have more than one-third acre (6 billion people, less than 1.5 billion families). Federal forests take up about 25% of U.S. area. (SA)

REFERENCES

(CI)   CIA statistics, 1992 (statistics published annually and available in most university libraries)
(DI)   Webster's New School and Office Dictionary, 1960, p 885
(LU)   U.S. Government land utilization data
(ME)   (major encyclopedias and pocket dictionaries, figures will vary slightly.)
(MK)   K. M. Malin, Food Resources of the Earth, Vol 3 p 386, Proceedings of the World Population Conference, 1967
(SA)   US Statistical Abstract, any edition

CHAPTER 5

POPULATION HISTORY, BIRTH RATES, DEATH RATES, DENSITY, GROWTH

501 What do advocates of population control allege about population growth and birth rates?

502 What do opponents of population control allege about population growth and birth rates?

503 How can we determine if population controllers or their opponents are correct about population trends?

504 What questions can be raised to determine if population will grow so fast that population control is or will soon be required?

505 Has population growth caused any problem sufficient to require population control?

506 Have world population growth rates and birth rates slowed substantially?

507 Why have birth rates decreased in developing countries?

508 How has China imposed population control?

509 Why have birth rates decreased when people have moved to cities?

510 Why do birth rates decrease when women become better educated?

511 Why do birth rates decrease when women work outside of the home?

512 Have birth rates declined because the death rate declined?

513 Have birth rates declined as average income has increased?

514 What can we say about future population growth in developed countries?

515 What can we say about future population growth in developing countries?

516 If the birth rate has been dropping, why is the rate of population increase still 1.7%?

517 Give details about world and region population, rate of increase, birth rate, area, and population density.

518 What are the area, population and density of each state?

519 What are the population and population density of each of the 25 largest U.S. city metropolitan areas?

520 What are the most populous countries?

521 Where are people most likely to live under crowded urban conditions, in Australia, Canada, China, or India?

501 What do advocates of population control allege about population growth and birth rates?

Population control advocates allege:

a) We are having a population explosion.

49

b) Population grows exponentially so it must be stopped now, because if we do approach a crisis of too many people, by the time we see the problem it will be too late.

c) Unless we have population control, disastrous overcrowding is inevitable because people will have too many babies.

d) There is no evidence that population growth is stopping, even though birth rates are going down.

e) Population growth is so fast that it causes many problems, and these problems can be solved only by stopping population growth.

502 What do opponents of population control allege about population growth and birth rates?

a) Population is growing at a rate of less than 2% per year (UN estimates 1.7% per year) (DY), so population is not exploding.

b) This 1.7% annual growth is so slow that any problems can be foreseen a long time before they become critical, particularly since major problems population controllers have used as justification for population control have become less serious with time.

c) A substantial amount of the population growth rate has been caused by a reduction in death rate. Every major population growth rate trend points to a stoppage of population growth relatively soon followed immediately by a reduction in population which will cause severe problems.

d) The number of births in the world is expected to decrease every year after the year 2000. (SW18)

e) In every major way, population growth of the past fifty years has been associated with a reduction in the severity of problems faced by the human race and an increase in quality of life. (See other chapters of this book for details.)

503 How can we determine if population controllers or their opponents are correct about population trends?

a) Look at present population trends;

b) look at the future changes that will alter present population trends so that you can predict future population trends.

504 What questions can be raised to determine if population will grow so fast that population control is or will soon be required?

a) Has population growth caused any problem sufficient to require population control?

b) Have world birth rates decreased?

c) Why have birth rates decreased in developing countries?

d) Have birth rates decreased when people have moved to cities?

e) Have birth rates decreased when women have become better educated?

f) Have birth rates decreased when women have become more likely to work outside of the home?

g) Have birth rates declined as the chance of each baby living increased?

h) Have birth rates declined as average income has increased?

i) Is it true that world births are expected to decline every year after 2000?

505 Has population growth caused any problem sufficient to require population control?

No. Major alleged problems are discussed in other chapters of this book. Population growth has been shown to be associated in about 50 ways with improved quality of life.

506 Have world population growth rates and birth rates decreased substantially?

Yes. Before 1970, the world population growth rate was about 2% annually. Since the 1970's, the world population growth rate has declined to 1.7% annually and it is expected to go substantially lower. World population growth rate equals birth rate minus death rate. (DYv) Birth rates have decreased as shown in Table 5-1, and are expected to continue to decline.

Countries	1991 Population (millions)	Birth Rate 1960	Birth Rate 1991	Death Rate 1960	Death Rate 1991	Fertility Rate 1991	Population Growth Rate 1960	Population Growth Rate 1991
Least Dev.	519	48	44	25	16	6.0	2.3%	2.8%
Developing	4147	42	30	20	9	3.7	2.2%	2.1%
Developed	1213	21	14	9	10	1.9	1.2%	0.4%
(SW69, 77)								

507 Why have birth rates decreased in developing countries?

Birth rates have decreased in developing countries primarily because life expectancy has improved, meaning that parents do not need two sons to have an expectation that one son will survive to provide for them in their old age.

The UN Food and Agriculture Organization analyzed the relationship as follows: "Poverty and *rapid population growth* reinforce each other in a number of ways. Low wages, inadequate education (especially among women) and high infant mortality—all linked to poverty—contribute to high fertility rates and thus to rapid population growth." (SF137)

In addition, many millions of people have moved to cities where economic factors change so that additional children do not help family finances. Further, women on average are becoming more educated and more likely to work outside the home, thereby reducing births. (DYv) (SYv)

Birth prevention is aggressively encouraged by government and school clinics and programs. In some nations, such as China, severe population control measures have been imposed. (BE) In most nations, the media have saturated the public with effective hedonistic, anti-baby, anti-traditional family propaganda, while frequently suppressing contrary viewpoints.

In addition to the above reasons, some developing countries have adopted the U.S. concept of penalizing parenthood via taxes. In the 1950's, a U.S. family of four with average income paid essentially no income or social security tax. In the 1990's, such a family would have to pay about $10,000 annually. To penalize marriage, married people have a higher tax rate than two single people with the same incomes who are living together.

508 How has China imposed population control?

In the case of China, population control has meant:

a) imposition of a one-child policy with serious penalties for an average couple having one or more children;

b) millions of baby girls killed so that the one permitted child will be a boy;

c) forced sterilization;

d) forced abortions of many women who without government permission dared to become pregnant a second time;

e) monthly forced examination of women of childbearing age to make certain they are not pregnant a second time, and if they are pregnant, to forcefully impose abortion;

f) imposition of severe penalties on couples who do not cooperate with the one-child policy. (BE)

509 Why have birth rates decreased when people have moved to cities?

In the countryside in developing countries, each child slightly decreases the family standard of living until the child is about seven years old, but after the age of seven, the work done by the child exceeds in value the cost of providing for it so that having more children improves family living standards. In cities, few children find work, so each child on average reduces family living standards. Parents, accordingly, have fewer children. (PG)

In U.S. cities, large families can find big enough homes and cars. In other countries, including countries in Europe, affordable homes and cars are very small, so parents have to choose between having large families or a typical city life. Most decide not to have large families.

510 Why do birth rates decrease when women become better educated?

If women have their first child at a later age, they are likely to have fewer children. Better-educated women spend more time in school and therefore usually have their first child at a later age. Until recently, about half the women in the world lived in the subsistence agricultural economy of developing countries, where mos children have meant better living standards. Increasing education has changed conditions so that more children mean financial sacrifice. Accordingly, better-educated people have frequently had fewer children. Better-educated women seeking employment outside the home on average have fewer children.

511 Why do birth rates decrease when women work outside of the home?

Employment outside the home is usually associated with smaller families because it gives the woman responsibilities and opportunities which decrease the factors that lead people to have children.

512 Have birth rates declined because the death rate declined?

Yes. Average people in developing countries have no old-age security other than the earning capacity of their sons. If a couple had one son and he died, they could starve. With high death rates, many children died young, and it was prudent to have two or three sons in the hope that at least one would survive until old age. With lower child mortality rates, many couples stop having babies after a first son.

513 Have birth rates declined as average income has increased?

Yes. Developing countries' per capita income has increased more than 100% since 1948. (SY79) Improved material standards permit families to seek pleasures not associated with and sometimes contradictory to large families.

514 What can we say about future population growth in developed countries?

A fertility rate of about 2.2 births per woman is needed to maintain a country's population. The calculation is as follows: two children replace two parents; .2 children replace those who die childless. In 1991, no developed country had a fertility rate high enough for its population to grow. The people of the developed countries will gradually diminish in number as soon as those born in the 1950's become old enough to have high death rates. (SW77)

515 What can we say about future population growth in developing countries?

In the 1990's, the actual number being born in developing countries will be less than previously in every area of the world except Africa and South Asia. By about the year 2000, the total number of births in the developing countries is projected to begin to decrease so that the births from 2001 to 2010 will be less than world births from 1991 to 2000. If this continues, then before today's young people become old, earth's population will decline.

Projected changes in numbers of births are as follows: births in Latin America will decrease by about 100,000 between 1993 and 2003. In South Asia, births will decrease by 3 million from 2003 to 2015. In East Asia, births will drop about 5.6 million from 1993 to 2002. In Africa births will continue to increase. (SW18)

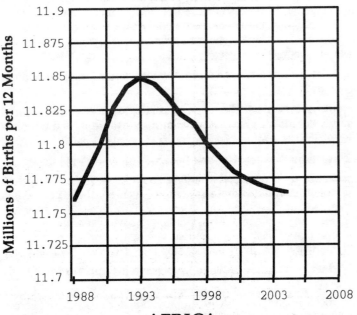

LATIN AMERICA

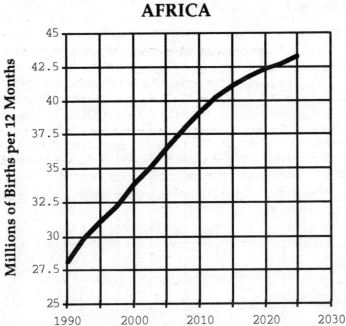

AFRICA

(The graphs of projected number of births are only projections by the United Nations based on data known in 1993, and may not accurately predict what will actually happen.)

SOUTH ASIA

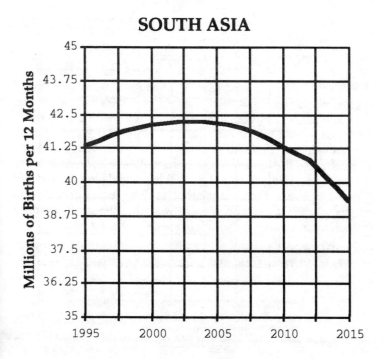

EAST ASIA

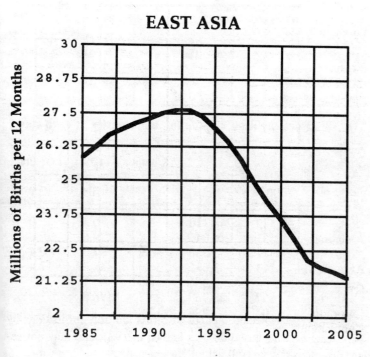

516 If the birth rate has been dropping, why is the rate of population increase still 1.7%?

Life expectancy in developing countries improved from 46 to 61 years between 1960 and 1991, while the death rate was cut from 20 to 9 per thousand per year. (SW77) The rate of population growth is the birth rate minus the death rate. In the 1950's and 1960's, both birth and death rates were higher. Typical rates were a birth rate of 3.3% and a death rate of 1.3% with a 3.3% - 1.3% = 2.0% population growth rate. In 1990, in comparison, population growth was 1.7% because the birth rate was estimated to be 1.7% higher than the death rate. The birth rate predicts future population growth rates, because everyone born eventually dies. The recent drop in birth rate indicates that the population growth rate will drop, probably to the point that population will decrease by about the year 2050.

517 Give details about world and region population, rate of increase, birth rate, area, and population density.

year	Population (millions) 1950	1960	1970	1980	1990	1985-90 Annual % Rate of Increase	1985-90 Birth Rate	Death Rate	Area (1000 km²⁾	Population Density per km²
World	2,516	3,020	3,698	4,448	5,292	1.7	27	10	136,255	39
Africa	222	279	362	477	642	3.0	45	15	30,305	22
Asia	1,377	1,668	2,102	2,583	3,171	1.9	28	9	27,582	115
Latin Amer.	166	218	286	363	448	2.1	29	7	20,535	22
North Amer.	166	199	226	252	278	0.8	15	9	21,962	13
Europe	393	425	460	484	498	0.2	13	11	4,933	101
Oceania	12.6	15.8	19.3	22.8	26.5	1.5	19	8	8,536	3
Former USSR	180	214	243	266	289	0.8	18	11	22,402	13

(USSR not included in Asia or Europe) (DY)

518 What are the area, population and density of each state?

State	Land Area (1000 mi)	1990 Census (1000s)	Change %	Persons Per Sq Mile	Persons Per Sq Km
USA	3,549	248,710	9.8	70.3	27.0
Alabama	51	4,041	3.8	79.6	30.6
Alaska	571	550	36.9	1.0	0.4
Arizona	114	3,665	34.8	32.3	12.4
Arkansas	52	2,351	2.8	45.1	17.3
California	157	29,760	25.7	190.8	73.4
Colorado	104	3,294	14.0	31.8	12.2
Connecticut	5	3,287	5.8	678.4	260.9
Delaware	2	666	12.1	340.8	131.1

(Continued'

56

State	Land Area (1000 mi)	1990 Census (1000s)	Change %	Persons Per Sq Mile	Persons Per Sq Km
D.C.	0.06	607	-4.9	9,882.8	3801.1
Florida	58	12,938	32.7	239.6	92.2
Georgia	58	6,478	18.6	111.9	43.0
Hawaii	6	1,108	14.9	172.5	66.6
Idaho	83	1,007	6.7	12.2	4.7
Illinois	56	11,431	0	205.6	79.1
Indiana	36	5,544	1.0	154.6	59.7
Iowa	56	2,777	-4.7	49.7	19.2
Kansas	82	2,478	4.8	30.3	11.7
Kentucky	40	3,685	0.7	92.8	35.8
Louisiana	45	4,220	0.3	96.9	37.4
Maine	31	1,228	9.2	39.8	15.4
Maryland	10	4,781	13.4	489.2	188.9
Massachusetts	8	6,016	4.9	767.6	296.4
Michigan	57	9,295	0.4	163.6	63.2
Minnesota	84	4,375	7.3	55.0	21.2
Mississippi	47	2,573	2.1	54.9	21.2
Missouri	69	5,117	4.1	74.3	28.7
Montana	146	799	1.6	5.5	2.1
Nebraska	77	1,578	0.5	20.5	7.9
Nevada	110	1,202	50.1	10.9	4.2
New Hampshire	9	1,109	20.5	123.7	47.8
New Jersey	8	7,730	5.0	1,042.0	402.3
New Mexico	122	1,515	16.3	12.5	4.8
New York	50	17,990	2.5	381.0	147.1
N. Carolina	49	6,629	12.7	136.1	52.6
N. Dakota	69	639	-2.1	9.3	3.6
Ohio	41	10,847	0.5	264.9	102.3
Oklahoma	69	3,146	4.0	45.8	17.7
Oregon	96	2,842	7.9	29.6	11.4
Pennsylvania	45	11,882	0.1	265.1	102.4
Rhode Island	1	1,003	5.9	960.3	370.8
S. Carolina	30	3,487	11.7	115.8	44.7
S. Dakota	76	696	0.8	9.2	3.6
Tennessee	42	4,877	6.2	118.3	45.7
Texas	263	16,987	19.4	64.9	25.1
Utah	82	1,723	17.9	21.0	8.1
Vermont	9	563	10.0	60.8	23.5
Virginia	40	6,187	15.7	156.3	60.3
Washington	67	4,867	17.8	73.1	28.2
West Virginia	24	1,793	-8.0	74.5	28.8
Wisconsin	55	4,892	4.0	90.1	34.8
Wyoming	97	454	-3.4	4.7	1.8

USC)

519 What are the population and population density of each of the 25 largest U.S. city metropolitan areas?

Cities metropolitan area	1990 Census (millions)	Pop Density (per sq mi)	Area (sq mi)
New York	17.953	2,353.8	763
Los Angeles	14.532	427.8	3397
Chicago	8.066	1,435.5	562
San Francisco	6.253	848.6	737
Philadelphia	5.899	1,103.6	535
Detroit	4.665	901.4	518
Washington, DC	3.924	989.1	397
Dallas	3.885	557.7	697
Boston	3.784	1,550.5	244
Houston	3.711	522.1	711
Miami	3.193	1,012.4	315
Atlanta	2.833	553.3	512
Cleveland	2.760	948.4	291
Seattle	2.559	434.4	589
San Diego	2.498	594.1	420
Minneapolis	2.464	487.8	505
St Louis	2.444	458.5	533
Baltimore	2.382	913.0	261
Pittsburgh	2.243	584.8	384
Phoenix	2.122	230.6	920
Tampa	2.068	809.5	255
Denver	1.848	410.4	450
Cincinnati	1.744	672.8	259
Milwaukee	1.607	896.3	179
Kansas City (USC)	1.566	314.0	499

520 What are the most populous countries?

Country	Population (millions)	Area (thousands) mi²	Area (thousands) km²	Population Density mi²	Population Density km²
1. China	1,155	3,678	9,527	314	121
2. India	849	1,269	3,287	669	258
3. USA	252	3,619	9,372	70	27
4. Indonesia	187	741	1,919	252	97
5. Brazil	153	3,286	8,512	47	18
6. Russia	148	6,593	17,075	22	9
7. Japan	123	146	378	842	325
8. Bangladesh	118	56	140	2107	843
9. Pakistan	115	310	804	371	143
10. Nigeria	112	356	924	315	121
11. Mexico	87	758	1,964	115	44
12. Germany	80	138	357	580	224
13. Vietnam	68	127	329	535	207
14. Philippines	62	116	300	534	207
15. Turkey	60	301	781	199	77
16. UK (Britain)	57	94	244	606	234
17. Italy	57	116	301	491	189
18. France	57	211	547	270	104
19. Thailand	56	198	514	283	109
20. Iran	55	636	1,648	86	33
21. Egypt	54	387	1,001	140	54
22. Ethiopia	53	472	1,222	112	43
23. Ukraine (DY)	52	232	603	224	86

521 Where are people most likely to live under crowded urban conditions, in Australia, Canada, China, or India?

The United Nations lists percentage urbanization as follows:

Country	% Urban
Australia	85.4
Canada	76.5
China	26.2
India	25.7

(DY136-145)

REFERENCES

(BE) Stephen Mosher, *Broken Earth* ((London: Robert Hale, 1983) gives many details and was instrumental in causing the U.S. government to cut off money to the UN used to fund China's Population Control program

(PG) Colin Clark, *Population Growth: The Advantages*

(DY) 1991 *UN Demographic Yearbook;* (v) means various years (DY)

(SF) *The State of Food and Agriculture*, 1991 UN Food and Agriculture Organization

(SW) *The State of the World's Children* 1993 by United Nations International Childrens Emergency Fund (UNICEF), Oxford University Press

(SY) *UN Statistical Yearbook*, published annually

(USC) 1990 US Census

CHAPTER 6

EXTINCTION OF SPECIES

601 What is a species?
602 What questions need to be answered to determine if population control advocates are correct when they claim widespread extinction of species?
603 According to the U.S. government how many species have become extinct since 1973?
604 How many species are listed by the U.S. government as having become endangered, i.e., in danger of becoming extinct?
605 How many species are listed by the U.S. government as in danger of becoming extinct over an area as small as 3% of their natural range?
606 How many species are listed as being threatened with extinction over 100% of their range?
607 How many species are listed by the U.S. government as threatened over as small an area as 3% of their range?
608 What has the U.S. government predicted about species extinction?
609 What is the *Global 2000* prediction of massive species extinction based on?
610 What evidence did Lovejoy give for his estimate of at least 500,000 species extinctions by the year 2000?
611 What value judgment does U.S. law accept to protect endangered species?
612 What do opponents of population control allege about species extinction?
613 How useful is the scientific definition of species?
614 How many species are there?
615 What percentage of species that have ever lived are already extinct?
616 Of the million known species, how many become extinct each year?
617 What is wrong with the scientific definition of species from the viewpoint of those claiming large numbers of species extinctions?
618 What is a subspecies?
619 Have those claiming that great numbers of species are becoming extinct adopted a non-scientific definition of species thereby inflating the number of species becoming extinct?
620 How many subspecies are there which may be called species by the political, anti-scientific definition of species?
621 How do some population control advocates and ecologists determine the number of species they claim are going extinct?
622 What is lost when a species is lost?
623 How many new species are formed each year?

601 What is a species?

"A species is a group of more or less distinct organisms (ie. plants, or animals) that are capable of interbreeding with one another in the wild, but are reproductively isolated from other species . . . Organisms that reproduce asexually (without mating) are classified into species on the basis of morphological and biochemical characteristics." (B2p455)

602 What questions need to be answered to determine if population control advocates are correct when they claim widespread extinction of species?

a) What is a species?

b) Of the known species, how many become extinct each year?

c) How many species are alleged to be lost each year?

d) Have those claiming that great numbers of species are becoming extinct adopted a non-scientific definition of species which inflates the number of species becoming extinct?

e) Have those claiming that great numbers of species are becoming extinct adopted a non-scientific method of calculating the number of species becoming extinct?

f) What is lost when a species is lost?

g) What is the evidence that supports the allegation that large numbers of species become extinct each year?

h) How many species are listed as extinct, threatened and endangered by the U.S. government?

603 According to the U.S. government, how many species have become extinct since 1973?

Seven species have been delisted, which means they are believed to have become extinct during the 20-year period between 1973 and 1993. Six more species are believed to have possibly become extinct, but the extinction has not been sufficiently confirmed so that the six can be delisted. (FW phone call)

604 How many species are listed by the U.S. government as having become endangered, i.e., in danger of becoming extinct?

To the author's knowledge, none. The U.S. government defines endangered as "in danger of becoming extinct." The author knows of no government publication, U.S., UN or any other government, that lists species in danger of extinction. What is listed is the number of species endangered over part of their natural range.

605 How many species are listed by the U.S. government as in danger of becoming extinct over an area as small as 3% of their natural range?

The definition used by the U.S. government is: "Endangered species: One in danger of becoming extinct throughout all or a significant part of its natural range." The Oregon spotted owl range is about 3% of total spotted owl range and the spotted owl is listed, so 3% of a species range is sufficient for it to be considered endangered. In 1991, 974 species were listed as endangered. (FW) As of the writing of this book, there has been no official announcement known to the author indicating any of the 974 have become extinct.

606 How many species are listed as being threatened with extinction over 100% of their range?

To the author's knowledge, none. The U.S. government defines "threatened" as "One likely to become endangered in the foreseeable future," but endangered means in as little as 3% or less of its range. The author knows of no government publication, U.S., UN, or any other government, that lists species threatened with extinction.

607 How many species are listed by the U.S. government as threatened over as small an area as 3% of their range?

Using the definition "Threatened species: one likely to become endangered in the foreseeable future" (over as little as 3% of their range), the U.S. government lists 193 species as threatened. (FW)

608 What has the U.S. government predicted about species extinction?

The U.S. government has published as fact in *The Global 2000 Report to the President* the unverified speculation of one author who contended without any evidence that "Extinctions of plant and animal species will increase dramatically. Hundreds of thousands of species—perhaps as many as 20% of all species on earth—will be irretrievably lost as their habitats vanish, especially in tropical forests." (G2 I p 3)

609 What is the *Global 2000* prediction of massive species extinction based on?

Global 2000 relies only on the following summary of a table and statements by author Lovejoy:

"What then is a reasonable estimate of global extinctions by 2000? Given the amount of tropical forest already lost (which is important but often ignored), the extinctions can be estimated. . . . In the low deforestation case, approximately 15% of the planet's species can be expected to be lost. In the high deforestation case, perhaps as many as 20% will be lost. This means that of the 3-10 million species now present on earth, at least 500,000 to 600,000 will be extinguished during the next two decades" (1980-2000). (G2 II p 331)

610 What evidence did Lovejoy give for his estimate of at least 500,000 species extinctions by the year 2000?

Lovejoy gave no scientific evidence. The only published source given by Lovejoy for his key table (G2 II Table 13-30, p 331) is *The Sinking Ark* by Myers (1979), summarized as follows:

(1) The estimated extinction rate of known species is about one every four years between 1600 and 1900.

(2) The estimated rate is about one a year from 1900 to the present.

No sources or evidence are given by Myers for the two preceding estimates.

(3) Some scientists have "hazarded a guess" that the extinction rate "could now have reached" 100 species per year. That is, the estimate is simply conjecture and is an upper limit for the greatest possible number of extinctions.

The upper limit in (3) was made, then, without any basis in fact, arbitrarily multiplied by a factor of several hundreds and used by Myers, and then by Lovejoy, and then by *Global 2000* as the basis for the projection of 500,000 species becoming extinct in the twenty years 1980-2000. *Global 2000* published the 500,000 estimate as fact, and the media gave massive publicity to the estimate so that, with no contrary data publicized, it became accepted as fact.

611 What value judgment does U.S. law accept to protect endangered species?

According to U.S. law, to prevent massive extinction of species we must prevent destruction of any substantial habitat. This basically means that no development can be allowed in areas where a threatened species is thought to live. (US) Each species is important in that it has a genetic code which, if lost, is possibly lost forever. Each of these genetic codes may be the source of something precious, such as a new medicine, and according to U.S. law, the potential loss of any species is so important that great expense and inconvenience must be endured rather than risking the loss of even one species. (US)

612 What do opponents of population control allege about species extinction?

The scare about species extinction has been manufactured in complete contradiction to scientific data. The highest proven rate of extinction is less than one species per year out of millions of species. If there have been massive species extinctions, there are a number of ways this could be proven, either by direct observation, or by indirect means such as a solid chain of empirical evidence. The fact that nobody has been able to prove substantial numbers of species extinctions indicates that there has been no widespread species extinction. Less than one species lost per year out of perhaps more than 20 million species is not a significant problem. Further, there is no evidence that the past loss of any species has caused humans any serious problems. While any loss of life is regrettable, protection of species habitats should be put in proper perspective with regards to other important human needs.

613 How useful is the scientific definition of species?

For scientific purposes, the definition of species is satisfactory. It is scientifically accurate and useful.

614 How many species are there?

Nobody knows. Most animal species are insects or other very small animals. Most species overall are probably plants, and most of these are very small. Substantially fewer than a million species have been catalogued, and estimates of the total number of scientific species vary between about one million and twenty million or more.

615 What percentage of species that have ever lived are already extinct?

Nobody knows. Estimates are that more than 99.9% of all species that have ever lived are already extinct.

616 Of the million known species, how many become extinct each year?

The total number of the million known species that is known to become extinct each year has been estimated to be less than one per year. (SL21)(FW)

617 What is wrong with the scientific definition of species from the viewpoint of those claiming large numbers of species extinctions?

The scientific definition of species makes it impossible to claim that a vast number of species are becoming extinct. Only a tricky, misleading definition of species, such as categorizing a subspecies as a species, permits one to claim extinction of large numbers of species.

618 What is a subspecies?

A subspecies is that part of a species in a location or which has an appearance or other selected trait which differs from other members of the species. Subspecies of humans include redheads or people from Arkansas who have moved to Washington, D.C., and among insects could include termites who happen to live in one house. Some may believe that calling the termites in a house a subspecies is extreme, but over several years, the number of termites in even one house may exceed the number of spotted owls in Oregon. Once one says that a subspecies can be defined by location, the potential number of subspecies can become very large, and one cannot logically deny the name "subspecies" to any readily defined group of any species.

619 Have those claiming that great numbers of species are becoming extinct adopted a non-scientific definition of species thereby inflating the number of species becoming extinct?

When population controllers say that a certain number of species are at risk or have become extinct, they ordinarily mean a subspecies, but they talk as if the subspecies is the entire species.

620 How many subspecies are there which may be called species by the political, anti-scientific definition of species?

The number of subspecies depends on the number of species and the ways you divide the species. For example, the spotted owl is spread over most of North America from Canada to Mexico. Some of these spotted owls live in Oregon. The approximately 3% of the spotted owls living in Oregon were defined for political purposes as a separate species, even though scientifically they are not. The spotted owl was then used as a justification for preventing logging, thereby crippling the Oregon timber industry. In this case, those who redefined the Oregon spotted owl showed that one can multiply the number of species by thirty. They divide the scientific species habitat into different artificially defined areas and call essentially identical birds in each area a separate species.

Nothing except common sense by others can stop population controllers from additionally dividing scientific species in other ways. Otherwise, by their unscientific way of defining species, we may soon have billions or even trillions of sub-species defined for political but not scientific purposes as species.

621 How do some population control advocates and ecologists determine the number of species they claim are going extinct?

Apparently, some population control advocates and ecologists first determine the number that will cause the public to react as desired, then find a way to calculate that number. They certainly do not count or use any other scientific system of measurement. For example, they may assume that as an area changes, 90% of the habitat changes, thereby making extinct 50% of the species that lived there before the change. They then guess the number of species that might have lived there, which gives them a number and some calculations that might make the number seem reasonable to someone who does not understand how the guess is made.

622 What is lost when a species is lost?

Scientifically, genetic material found only in that species may be lost. The loss of a species also removes that species from interactions in the ecology where that species formerly lived. With genetic engineering, however, new species are being developed. Genetically engineered medicines and a tomato, for example, have been approved for sale to the public.

Some who claim massive species extinction apparently believe in a form of pantheism or nature worship. (FO) They allege that humans are not different in kind or superior in quality to other species. For them, the loss of a subspecies such as the spotted owl in Oregon may appear to be as evil as the extinction of the human race. Some regard humans as a cancer on the earth. (PB Prologue) For these, population control or even the loss of the entire human race might be considered good, since it would make more room for other species.

Others see scientific species loss as a tragic and regrettable loss of life, but do not see this loss as justification for the elimination of human beings. They believe remedies other than population control can be applied.

623 How many new species are formed each year?

Each year hundreds of new species thought to be valuable are formed by genetic engineering.

REFERENCES

(B2) Claude A. Villee, *Biology*, 2nd Ed., Harvard University et al. (1989) Saunders College Publishing
(DI) *Worldbook Dictionary*, 1986, Doubleday & Co. Inc.
(FO) Speech on population of Jane Fonda (wife of Ted Turner, head of CNN and long-time promoter of population control) to the United Nations, Sept 20, 1993. This speech praised President Clinton and presumably was made with his approval
(FW) Pursuant to U.S. law, the Fish and Wildlife Department is the U.S. government agency that keeps track of known species and delists any species that becomes extinct. (FW) refers to information given the author by telephone by the Fish and Wildlife Department.
(G2) *Global 2000 Report to the President* (1980) (President Carter)
(PB) Paul Ehrlich, *Population Bomb*, (1968) Ballantine Books, NY
(SA) Myers, *The Sinking Ark*, (1979), as quoted in (G2)
(SL) Julian L Simon and Aaron Wildavsky, *Species Loss Revisited*, (1993)
(US) U.S. law passed by Congress and now in effect. This law has caused the closing of much of the U.S. timber industry in Washington and Oregon, resulting in the loss of thousands of jobs and the highest U.S. timber prices in history. Examples of many billions of dollars of development lost with loss of thousands of jobs in construction and more thousands of potential jobs in the never developed areas periodically make the news. So far the species protected have frequently been subspecies never heard of before and found in quantity elsewhere

CHAPTER 7

POLLUTION SOLUTION

Population control advocates claim more people necessarily generate more pollution. (PB) (LG) Opponents allege that the environment can be kept clean regardless of population if we make appropriate efforts to clean the environment.

Controlling pollution requires money, whether to pay for low technology work such as garbage collection, or high technology work such as air quality monitoring. Developed countries have been able to spend sufficient money to accomplish most pollution control goals. Developing countries, with less money, have had to make hard choices and have tolerated higher levels of pollution. The economies of developing countries are advancing very fast, and as more money becomes available, developing countries will probably choose to spend more to control pollution. For example, not too long ago, all developing countries had unsafe water. Fortunately, as technology advances, it becomes less costly to control pollution. In 1990, most people in developing countries had safe water. (SW73) Progress is being made. Let us hope it will be made quickly.

Discussion of pollution problems in alphabetical order follows.

701 Acid rain.

From about 1970 to 1990, environmental activists warned us that thousands of lakes had been killed and thousands more were at risk. "The EPA announced in 1980 that the average acidity of northeast US lakes had increased a hundredfold over the past forty years. No evidence was cited to support this position. In 1981, the National Research Council joined in with a forecast that the number of acidified lakes would double by 1990....It is now known that the 'acidified lakes' have simply returned to their pre-Industrial Age condition. During the 19th century, extensive logging and slash burning had added quantities of alkaline ash to the watershed, countering the natural acidity of the surrounding soil and water. With cessation of these activities, the lakes and rivers of the northeast have simply reverted to their natural state....By 1980, Congress responded to all this hype by authorizing a ten-year $500 million dollar study, which became known as the National Acid Precipitation Assessment Project (NAPAP)....The NAPAP study found that of more than 7,000 northeastern lakes, only 240 were acidic; the average lake has just about the same degree of acidity as before the industrial Era....When asked what would happen to lake and stream acidity if no actions were taken over the next 50 years, Dr. James Mahoney, the director of NAPAP from 1987 to 1990, said, 'Nothing.'" (EO147-149)

702 Air Pollution

Throughout the world, where efforts have been made to reduce air pollution, air pollution has been reduced. (SYv) This decrease in air pollution has been more or less continual in the US and wherever substantial efforts have been made since about 1960. For example, between 1969 and 1975, the EPA announced that total air pollution in the US declined from 240 million tons to 200 million tons. Please see this chapter, entries on acid rain, carbon dioxide, carbon monoxide, nitrous oxides, particulates, smog, and sulfur oxides and the following table for additional information.

Air Quality, U.S.

air QS	1982	1983	1984	1985	1986	1987	1988	1989	1990
Pollutant									
Carbon dioxide	9	7.95	7.82	7.74	6.99	7.11	6.67	6.42	6.32 5.89
Ozone	.120	.125	.137	.125	.123	.119	.125	.136	.116 .114
Sulfur dioxide	.030	.010	.009	.010	.009	.009	.009	.009	.008 .008
Particulates	75	48.7	48.4	49.9	47.7	47.6	48.6	49.7	48.0 47.3
Nitrogen dioxide	.053	.024	.023	.024	.024	.024	.024	.024	.023 .022
Lead	1.500	.484	.413	.381	.258	.151	.108	.087	.074 .070

air QS= National Ambient Air Quality Standard

Lead is greatly diminished because of a switch to unleaded gasoline. Other pollutants have been kept substantially below National Ambient Air Quality Standard, with the most recent years being the cleanest and best for average air quality, on average more than twice as clean as the National Ambient Air Quality Standard set by the U.S. Government Environmental Protection Agency. (EPt)

air pollution, U.S. 1970-1990 millions of metric tons of pollutants released				
Pollutant year	1970	1980	1990	% change 1980-1990
Carbon monoxide	101.4	79.6	60.1	24% less
Sulfur Oxides	28.4	23.4	21.2	9% less
Volatile Organic Compounds	25.0	21.1	18.7	11% less
Particulates	18.5	8.5	7.5	12% less
Nitrogen Oxides	18.5	20.9	19.6	6% less
Lead	0.204	0.071	0.007	90% less

Reduction in total pollutants, 1970 to 1990, 64.9 million metric tons, a 34% reduction. Reduction in total amount of pollutants, 1940 to 1990, approximately 20 million tons. (EPe)

703 Air pollution (natural)

From natural sources. For example, in 1883, one volcano put nearly five cubic miles of crushed rock into the air and also put other pollution into the air. (KR) That is about 30 billion tons of air pollution, in less than a week from one volcano, probably more than man has put into the air during all his history. Argonne National Laboratory scientists estimate chlorophyll produces 100 million tons of carbon monoxide annually. (IA)

"The scientists found no evidence that human pollution came close to matching nature's." In fact, the air on earth actually got cleaner between 1963 and 1970. In 1963 Mt. Agung on Bali erupted cutting off more than five percent of the sunlight at the South Pole, many thousands of miles away. It took seven years for the atmosphere to return to normal. (DN)

When prominent geologists get together they agree "that man's contribution to air pollution in a global, long-term sense doesn't amount to much. On a geologic scale, it's unlikely that modern civilization will register much impact on the environment...19th Century volcanoes, to say nothing of earlier ones since the planet's birth, dumped more dust and ash into the air than man's activities have throughout recorded history..." The National Oceanic and Atmospheric Administration (NOAA) reported recently that the 1969 Barbados Oceanographic and Meteorological Experiment disclosed that the atmosphere over the tropical Atlantic is far more polluted than had been thought. Sources of the pollution, it was discovered, was dust blown westward from Africa. The dust was so abundant at levels up to 16,000 feet that it affected aircraft engines." (LA)

704 Alar

Alar prevents the premature dropping of apples from trees. An environmental group, the Natural Resources Defense Council, prompted the CBS program 60 Minutes to air unsubstantiated charges that alar was a serious cancer risk to children. Without reasonable investigation, more of the media then gave vast publicity to the charge. Additional investigation finally showed that the allegations were false. (EO 174-175)

705 Asbestos

Breathing certain types of asbestos can cause cancer, asbestosis, and other illnesses. There are six types of asbestos. Blue asbestos, also known as crodicidolite, and brown asbestos are dangerous because their fibers are difficult to remove from the lungs. Blue and brown asbestos comprise less than 5% of US asbestos use, but have not been ordinarily used in buildings. Blue asbestos was used in World War II ships and in Kent cigarette filters.

Soft white asbestos, known as chrysotile is used in 95% of asbestos applications, including substantially all applications in buildings. There is evidence that white asbestos is not dangerous. In buildings using white asbestos, air concentrations of 0.001 fiber per cubic centimeter are typical, and life time exposure to concentrations of white asbestos thousands of times greater than 0.001 has failed to show any significant hazard. Also, the body is able to and routinely does remove white asbestos from the lungs.

Removing white asbestos from buildings usually increases the concentration of white asbestos in the air for a time to a level more than 1000 times greater than leaving it in place. Asbestos can be covered by paint to additionally reduce its concentration in the air.

Perhaps not understanding the preceding facts, the EPA has already caused more than 100 billion dollars to be spent to remove white asbestos from buildings. (EO151-156)

706 Cancer causing substances

"Careful studies have established that 99.99% of the carcinogenic materials injested daily are either natural or produced by drinking alcohol, cooking, or smoking." (TP77)

Please see Alar, Asbestos, Dioxins and PCBs.

707 Carbon dioxide (CO_2)

Please see Air pollution and Chapter 8, Global Warming. CO_2 is necessary for life and for plant growth.

708 Carbon monoxide

Release of carbon monoxide into the U.S. atmosphere declined from 101.4 million metric tons in 1970 to 79.6 million metric tons in 1980 to 60.1 million metric tons in 1990. Please see Air Pollution.

709 DDT

DDT has not been used in developed nations and has been used infrequently in developing nations for more than 20 years. DDT did not cause the alleged harm to birds or humans, was an effective insecticide, and in the environment soon broke down into harmless by-products under normal conditions. DDT lasted for a long time only where the soil was dark, dry, and devoid of microorganisms. Many experiments indicated that DDT did not thin egg shells, even when birds were fed 1000 times as much as they would eat under natural conditions. (TP68-77)

710 Dioxin

"Very small amounts of dioxin are fatal to guinea pigs. But the very same doses-and even doses 1,000 times greater have no deleterious effects on rats, mice, or any other laboratory animals on which dioxins have been tested, or, as far as we know, on man....As Dr. Vernon Houk of the Centers for Disease Control has said, 'Over the past eight years (1981-1989), the science base on human exposure to dioxin has expanded substantially....We know for certain that dioxin can cause chloracne...but as yet, we have found no other adverse health effect.'...A study conducted by the National Institute of Occupational Safety and Health showed that 5,200 workers with dioxin levels up to 200 times greater than the average U.S. exposure suffered no increase in cancer rates or any other health problem, save the skin rash." (EO142-143)

711 Disease

Except for sexually transmitted diseases, great progress is being made. Smallpox has been eliminated. UNICEF suggests that intensified vaccination efforts will soon eliminate other diseases such as polio. In the developed world, diseases which used to kill most people are now rare. In the developing countries, life expectancy is increasing about 6 months each year, by far the fastest improvement in history. Unfortunately, more could and should be done.

Major immunization now averages close to 80%, but should be made universal for certain diseases. 25 cents each worth of antibiotics would prevent more than a million child deaths annually from pneumonia. (SW4)

712 Electro-magnetic fields (EMF)
Every use of electricity causes EMF. EMF are an inescapable part of our environment, since the earth causes them by rotating. In addition, nature causes EMF via solar activity, lightning, and even the operation of the cells of our bodies. Since our cells use electricity, natural electric fields occur across cell membranes that are about 100 times greater than those generated by common man-made electricity use. EMF falls off very rapidly with distance. Research regarding EMF danger is not complete. Research has not yet shown that there is no risk, especially in the presence of extremely strong fields. (EO156-160)

713 Fertilizer
Improper use of fertilizer can cause salinization of soil. The average farmer knows how to fertilize without harming soil or watershed. The less knowledgeable farmers are usually willing to learn because fertilizing properly will benefit them. Proper fertilization includes not washing vast amounts of fertilizer off the land and into draining streams and rivers.

714 Freons
Please see Chapter 9 on Ozone.

715 Global warming
Please see Chapter 8 on Global Warming.

716 Hazardous waste
Please see Toxic Waste.

717 Insecticides
There is a great need for effective insecticides. "For every person, there are more than 300 million insects, 10,000 of which are from species that cause diseases or ruin food or fiber products." (SC)

The needless banning of DDT apparently caused millions of unnecessary deaths each year from malaria alone. In World War I, More soldiers died from insect born typhus than from bullets. In World War II, after DDT was used, no soldier died of typhus. Insecticides can be used without harming the environment, are necessary to maintain modern high yield agriculture and to prevent disease. (TP68-77)

It has long been possible to get results from slow release insecticides. "According to N.F. Cardelli, chief scientist at the Creative Biology Laboratory in Larberton, Ohio, and a professor at the University of Akron, the amount of chemical needed in the slow release method will probably never be more than 3% of the present conventional applications, and may be as little as 1/10 of 1%." (CA)

Genetic research has begun to produce plants that can resist pests.

718 Nitrogen and nitrous oxide
Please see Fertilizer and Air pollution.

719 Noise
Noise is measured in decibels, a quantitative measure of sound pressure. The scale begins at 0 db which is the weakest sound that can be picked up by the healthy human ear. The scale is in logarithmic form. High pitched tones are more annoying, and thus are generally given more weight. The most common weighting system is the "A" scale written: dbA. Some sample noise readings in the dbA scale at distances which people are commonly exposed are:

Rustling leaves	20 dbA
Residential recommendation	
(N.Y. Task Force) Night	30 dbA
Day	40 dbA
Window air conditioner	55 dbA
Conversational speech	60 dbA
One automobile	up to 70 dbA
Beginning of hearing damage if prolonged	85 dbA
San Francisco quiet subway	85 dbA
New York recommendation maximum noise level in busy areas	85 dbA
Heavy city traffic	90 dbA
U.S. Kitchen, maximum	90 dbA
Truck or bus	up to 95 dbA
Home lawnmower	98 dbA
New York subway	102 dbA
Jet airliner (500 ft. overhead)	115 dbA
Human pain threshold	120 dbA
Rock Band, maximum	130 dbA
Rats killed by prolonged exposure	150 dbA
Saturn V moon rocket first stage	180 dbA

The solution to noise pollution is better design and maintenance of machines. Much progress has been made, but because noise pollution has not been emphasized as much as other problems, it has not been given great emphasis.

720 Oil Spills

Oil spills, in and around US water		
year	incidents	gallons
1975	10,998	21,528,444
1980	9,886	12,638,848
1981	9,589	8,919,789
1982	9,416	10,404,646
1983	10,530	8,378,719
1984	10,089	19,007,332
1985	7,740	8,465,055
1986	6,539	4,613,387
1987	6,352	3,887,004
1988	6,791	6,645,985
1989	8,225	13,615,706
1990	7,114	4,255,308(EP)

The trend in US oil spills is toward fewer spills and fewer gallons of oil spilled. Later investigation has indicated much less harm than previously feared from previous widely publicized oil spills. (EP)

721 Ozone

Ozone at ground level is a pollutant and decreased 11% between 1982/83 and 1989/90. Please see air pollution for more details. Ozone at very high levels absorbs harmful ultra-violet B radiation. Please see Ozone Chapter 9.

722 Particulates

In 1931, The U.S. Public Health Service found the average of particulates in the air in 14 cities was 510 micrograms per cubic meter (mg/m³). In 1957, the Department of Health Education and Welfare found 120 mg/m³. By 1969, particulates were only 92 mg/m³. By 1975, there was an additional 30% reduction followed by a further 10% reduction from 1980 to 1990. Please see Air pollution.

723 PCB's

Polychlorinated biphenyls (PCB's) are used as insulators in electric transformers. No adverse health effects were found in those working with PCB concentrations much greater than any exposure of the general public. In the early 1970's, the EPA announced that PCB's could break down to form dioxin and banned PCB's. (EO144) Please see dioxins.

724 Plastics

Please see trash. Plastics take up about 10% of landfill space. From 1977 to 1993, plastic milk jugs went from 98 to 60 grams. Other plastic containers were also reduced in weight. Reduction in weight means the container is easier to crush and comprises less waste. (NM26) Plastics can be made to be biodegradeable.

75

725 Pollution (historical)

"'The tendency,' said one historian, 'is to think the problem is unique to one's own time and place, to ignore the volumes of recorded history that show pollution-like those other present-day obsessions, lust and violence has always been with us.'

The social historians spoke of air pollution choking Londoners in the 14th century and of mercury poisoning killing Italians in the 18th century. They spoke of urban congestion in ancient Babylon, of man depleting the forests of 16th century Europe, of entire species of animals being destroyed long before the technological onslaughts of the 20th century. When you assume, as so many of the ecologists do, that the threat just began in the late 1960s, you run the risk of panic. 'There is some of that now, an edge of hysterical frenzy,' Weber says. 'Like all zeal for a good cause, it'll burn out in time, leaving the problem still to be solved.'

'But the problem will be worse than ever then, because the people will have been discouraged to the point of apathy by the doomsayers and the gap between the salvation they promised and the little they'll have actually achieved.'

Weber, an assistant professor of history, is particularly interested in this phenomenon as it relates to air pollution. 'Many Americans assume that smog first appeared in Los Angeles sometime in the late 1940s or early 1950s, and that it then spread across the country,' he says. In actuality, mining operations in England in the 13th and 14th centuries so polluted the London air that King Edward I, in 1307, issued a royal proclamation making the burning of coal while Parliament was in session a capital offense. One man was beheaded for ignoring that proclamation.

'Air pollution had become so severe in London by the 17th century that John Evelyn wrote a book lamenting: . . . that this Glorious and Ancient city...should so wrap her stately head in Clowds of Smoake and Sulphur, so full of Stink and Darknesse.' This pollution, Weber says, 'not only shortened life-expectancy in London, but injured vegetation and defaced buildings.'

'As the Industrial Revolution spread throughout Europe, pollution spread as well, and by the 20th century it had become an international dilemma. In the fog-bound Meuse Valley of Belgium, a temperature inversion layer over a heavily industrialized area killed more than 60 people in three days in 1930. In Donora, south of Pittsburgh, the same conditions killed 35 people in three months in 1948. And in London, with its coastal fog and the mist from its surrounding marshy bogs, air pollution killed 4,000 people in two weeks in 1952.'" (LT)

726 Radiation (radioactivity)

From nature, 40 trillion radioactive particles hit each person's body in a lifetime. That is an average of 15,000 radioactive particles each second. We don't feel them or suffer any apparent ill effect from this constant bombardment. (TP95)

Of the total radiation received by Americans, 82% comes from natural sources. Of the natural radiation, 55% of total radiation is from radon; 8% is from cosmic rays and solar radiation; 8% is from terrestrial sources, mostly uranium and thorium, and 11% comes from internal potassium 40.

Of the 18% that is man-made, 11% is from medical X-rays; nuclear medicine causes 4%; consumer products such as smoke detectors cause 3%; and all other sources cause 1%. The "other" category of 1% includes all radiation from the entire nuclear industry which causes no more than 0.1% (one part in a thousand) of our entire radiation exposure.

Radiation consists of alpha, beta, and gamma particles, and is the same, regardless of the source. (TP97)

Nuclear war would unleash vast amounts of deadly radioactivity. Poorly designed or maintained electricity generating nuclear reactors such as in Chernobyl can release large amounts of radioactivity. Developed nations have used reactors for years without Chernobyl type problems, and the claim is made that these reactors are safe. One hopes the claim is correct.

727 Smog

The word smog was first used in Los Angeles about 1940, and is a combination of smoke and fog. Substantial progress began to be made about 1960. Smog has been substantially reduced. Please see air pollution.

728 Sulfur oxides

Please see acid rain and air pollution.

729 Toxic waste

Wherever efforts have been made, toxic waste problems have diminished. Unfortunately, much bad science has controlled the cleanup, billions of dollars have been wasted, and much cleanup has not been done because money was wasted elsewhere. For details, see: (EO136-147).

730 Trash (solid waste)

Though there has been a gradual increase in the volume of trash, there is adequate landfill capacity. "Japan, a land poor country, has 24 operational sites. In the land rich U.S., there are only 4,800...We could put all the municipal solid waste of the U.S. for the next 1,000 years into an area 44 by 44 miles, an area less than one-tenth of 1% of the (lower 48 states) U.S. land area." (NM)

The important thing about trash is the cost of collecting it and getting rid of it safely. When inflation is considered, the cost of collecting and disposing of trash has decreased, indicating that trash is less of a problem than it used to be. In 1970, a truck with one driver and two men who would empty trash from the cans into the truck was typical. About 1980, compacting trucks came into general use, enabling each truck to carry more and therefore waste less time traveling to and from the dump site. About 1990, automation progressed with the use of standard large trash cans and automatic trash can lifting arms such as used in Phoenix. This enables one man to collect trash substantially faster than the three man truck in use in 1970, with great savings in labor costs.

Recycling has increased, but is still not significant in relation to the total amount of trash. Some experimental efforts to separate out certain things have been tried, but none is in wide use. Landfill and some incineration are the primary methods of disposal. In the US, 14% of trash is incinerated, compared to 60% incinerated in Japan. (NM26)

731 Ultraviolet light
Please see Chapter 9 on Ozone.

732 Water pollution, US
Violations of EPA water quality levels have been as follows:

Pollutant	Level	1980	1983	1984	1985	1986	1987	1988	1989	1990
Fecal bacteria	31	34	30	28	24	23	22	30	26
Dissolved Oxygen	5	4	3	3	3	2	2	3	2
Phosphorus	4	3	4	3	3	3	4	2	3
Lead	5	5	Z	Z	Z	Z	Z	Z	Z
Cadmium	1	1	Z	Z	Z	Z	Z	Z	Z

(GS) Z = less than 1

REFERENCES

(CA) Speaking at the 1971 meeting of the American Chemical Society, published in *Los Angeles Times*, 10/14/71, Pt.2 p10
(DN) *Detroit News*, 9/9/71, UPI Dispatch quoting US Commerce Department *National and Atmospheric Administration Report*
(EO) Dixy Lee Ray with Lou Guzzo, *Environmental Overkill*, (1993) Regnery Gateway, Washington DC
(EP) Environmental Protection Agency data
(EPe) National Air Pollution Emission Estimates, 1940-1990, March 1992
(EPt) National Air Quality and Emissions Trends Report, annual
(GS) US Geological Survey National Stream Quality Accounting Network
(IA) *Iron Age*, 7-72
(KR) "Krakatoa" in *Encyclopedia Brittanica*
(LA) *Los Angeles Times* 3/11/71, Pt1 Ap9
(LG) D.H.Meadows et al., *Limits to Growth: A Report for the Club of Rome's Project on the Predicament of Mankind*, (1972) Universe Books, NY
(LT) *Los Angeles Times* 6/70/71, Pt1p1
(NM) *New American Magazine*, Vol 8, #11, 6/1/92, Environmental Issue
(PB) Paul Ehrlich, *Population Bomb*, (1968) Ballantine Books, NY

(SC)   UPI article 3/28/74 quoting Dean Schniderman of the School of Biological Sciences of the U of California, Irvine, speaking to a meeting of the Entomological Society of America.

(SW)   *THE STATE OF THE WORLD'S CHILDREN 1993*, United Nations Children's Fund (UNICEF), Oxford University Press, Oxfordshire, UK

(SYv)   *UN Statistical Yearbook* published annually

(TP)   Dixy Lee Ray with Lou Guzzo, *Trashing the Planet*, (1990) Regnery Gateway, Washington, DC

CHAPTER 8

GLOBAL WARMING

801 Why do some express concern about global warming?

802 What is the response to these concerns about global warming?

803 What is the main thing to know about global warming?

804 Do most experts believe that global warming will be a problem?

805 Why would a great amount of global warming be important?

806 What is the best evidence for changes in earth's temperature?

807 What do earth surface measurements indicate?

808 Where has the greatest warming occurred?

809 How do scientists measure past earth temperature during years before there were thermometers?

810 How much has the earth warmed?

811 Why is 1881 so frequently used as the first year for world temperature comparisons?

812 Can the warming trend since the cold year 1881 be considered a return to normal?

813 Could global warming have been slowed because the oceans have to absorb much energy before the land and air can warm?

814 What are the ways energy can be transmitted through our atmosphere?

815 How does nature keep earth's average temperature about the same?

816 What is the greenhouse effect?

817 Why do greenhouse gases absorb radiated energy from the earth and fail to absorb radiated energy from the sun?

818 What is the main greenhouse gas?

819 Why do increases of greenhouse gases have little effect on earth's temperature?

820 Why is it important that carbon dioxide does not radiate to outer space from near earth's surface?

821 Why is substantially all water vapor found in the lowest four miles in the earth's atmosphere in contrast to other gases which are spread uniformly, and why is that important?

822 How much has CO_2 in the atmosphere increased?

823 How much is CO_2 projected to increase?

824 Why do some scientists doubt that atmospheric CO_2 concentration will ever double?

825 Do people produce other air pollution that tends to cool the earth?

826 Do volcanic eruptions change the temperature of the atmosphere?

827 What is the basis for allegations that global warming will exceed one degree Celsius?

828 How can we be certain that the computer models predicting greater atmospheric warming are incorrect?
829 What is the difference in average world temperature between the coldest and warmest years since 1881?
830 What energy is trapped by the greenhouse effect?
831 Did most of the warming since 1881 occur before the greenhouse effect could have caused it?
832 What is wrong with the predicted pattern of global warming?
833 What has apparently caused the 0.5 degree Celsius increase in temperature since 1881?

801 Why do some express concern about global warming?

a) Since 1881, there has been about a 0.5 degree Celsius increase in average world temperature.

b) The five hottest years since 1881 were in the 1980s.

c) The earth's greenhouse effect already increases the earth's temperature about 33 degrees Celsius, from nearly 20 degrees below zero to our present temperatures. Greenhouse gases in the atmosphere, except for water, have increased an average of more than 50% since the industrial revolution began and are still increasing. Those who allege concern about global warming allege that the increase in greenhouse gases has caused the 0.5 degree Celsius increase in temperature since 1881 and will magnify the present 33 degree Celsius greenhouse temperature increase to 36-38 degrees, thereby making the earth too warm.

d) All major greenhouse gases in the atmosphere except water are increasing. For example, CO_2 (carbon dioxide) is released by the burning of coal, petroleum and natural gas.

e) Computer models have indicated that a doubling of greenhouse gases, except for water, would cause an increase in average earth temperature of three to five degrees Celsius and an increase in ocean level of three to five feet caused by melting ice.

f) Government agencies such as the UN Intergovernmental Panel on Climate Change, (IPCC) have predicted that increasing greenhouse gases will increase earth's temperature by at least three degrees Celsius.

g) The amount of greenhouse gas increase is in terms of equivalent CO_2. An equivalent doubling of CO_2 is expected by IPCC approximately 2030. Because of the increase of other greenhouse gases, we are currently slightly more than half way to an effective doubling of CO_2 even though atmospheric CO_2 has only increased from about 280 parts per million (PPM) to about 355 PPM as of 1993. The difference between CO_2 and equivalent CO_2 is that equivalent CO_2 also includes warming caused by atmospheric gases other than water and CO_2, such as methane, freons and nitrogen compounds.

802 What is the response to these concerns about global warming?

a) True.

b) True.

c) The past increase in greenhouse gases and the 0.5 degrees increase in temperature are correct, but the 0.5 degree temperature increase is influenced by causes other than the increased greenhouse gases. The global warming scenario popularized by the media is impossible when the mechanics of atmospheric heat transfer is properly analyzed. Understanding what has changed during the 0.5 degree Celsius increase in average earth temperature indicates that there are other causes for the increase in temperature.

d) Experiments indicate that although the amount of atmospheric CO_2 is increasing, it will never double, because plants fertilized by the increased CO_2 will grow faster, and thus absorb the additional CO_2. (ID)

e) The atmosphere is far more complex than even the most intricate computer models. Consequently, computer models of atmospheric warming have been essentially useless, and their projections have been deceptive. If the computer models were reliable, there would already have been more than three times as much warming as has been experienced, and ocean levels would have risen substantially. Conversely, many things which have happened would have been impossible according to the computer models.

f) True. But according to the greenhouse warming theory which predicts massive additional greenhouse warming very soon, since we are more than half way to an effective doubling of CO_2, we should also have seen more than half the predicted massive additional greenhouse warming. This has not occurred, so the greenhouse warming theory must be incorrect.

Government departments and individuals who have alleged that massive global warming is coming are not those who best understand how the atmosphere transfers energy. Most atmospheric experts do not believe that substantial global warming is coming.

803 What is the main thing to know about global warming?

The evidence overwhelmingly indicates that there will not be significant warming in the earth's average temperature for two reasons:

1) Energy from the earth's surface is carried up above most of the atmosphere primarily by convection (upward air movement) of evaporated water, thus taking the energy up above the influence of increasing greenhouse gases.

2) The earth's greenhouse effect is already 93% effective in absorbing all outgoing radiation from earth's surface so that little additional greenhouse effect is possible. Earth differs from Venus

82

which has a massive greenhouse effect in that earth has massive amounts of water which bypasses much of the greenhouse effect and Venus does not. Water is evaporated (thereby absorbing massive amounts of energy) at the ocean surface, then carried up above nearly all greenhouse gases by rising air currents where it turns into rain, thereby releasing the evaporation energy where it can be radiated into space with no significant interference from greenhouse gases. (DV8)

804 Do most experts believe that global warming will be a problem?

Not most experts who understand how the atmosphere transfers energy. For purposes of this question, we define experts as the approximately 100 top atmospheric scientists in the world, since they best understand the atmosphere. These most knowledgeable experts do not believe that global warming is or will be a problem. Two of these experts have made the following evaluations: "This is why there is almost universal agreement among atmospheric scientists that little if any of the observed warming of the past century can be attributed to the man-induced increases in greenhouse gases." (SY53) "Indeed, a recent Gallup Poll of climate scientists (in the American Meteorological Society and in the American Geophysical Union) shows that a vast majority doubt that there has been any identifiable man-caused warming to date (49% said no, 33% didn't know, 18% thought yes some has occurred; however among those actively involved in research and publishing frequently in peer-reviewed research journals, 0% believe any man-caused global warming has occurred so far.)" (SC11), (ON 11)

There is a difference depending on specialty. A higher percentage of scientists who are climate modelers, chemists specializing in atmosphere chemistry and others not intimately involved with the details of the operation of the atmosphere claim to fear greenhouse warming. What they leave out of their calculations indicates they may misunderstand how the atmosphere transfers energy.

Like many population related problems, global warming is a battle between theory and data, with substantially all the data indicating there is no problem, but a number of people saying their theory indicates there should be a problem. The media usually gives much more coverage to those who say their theory indicates there is a problem, than to the data that says there is no such problem.

805 Why would a great amount of global warming be important?

It has been alleged that global warming of five degrees Celsius might raise the ocean level by up to five feet, increase droughts, and substantially reduce food production. None of these things have begun to happen or will happen.

806 What is the best evidence for changes in earth's temperature?

The best evidence for changes in earth's temperature comprises satellite observations. Satellites have measured earth's temperature since about 1979. One satellite takes temperature measurements of many thousands of times the atmospheric volume measured by earth surface measurements. The 15 years of satellite measurements (1979 to 1993) have indicated that some years have been warmer than others, but there has been no pattern of warming or cooling.(SC1558) 1992 and 1993 have been cooler than average years, and the stratosphere has been the coolest since perhaps the 1950's, possibly because of byproducts of the Mt Pinatubo volcanic eruption in the Philipines. (CW3)

807 What do earth surface measurements indicate?

Earth surface measurements, including balloon and non-satellite measurements of the earth's atmosphere, indicate an increase of about 0.5 degrees Celsius since 1881. This is usually regarded as a return to normal, not a warming, since the years around 1881 were so cold.

808 Where has the greatest warming occurred?

A US Department of Agriculture report indicates the only US warming since 1920 has been in the cities and that the countryside has cooled. "Temperatures in the US have decreased slightly over the past 70 years, a US Department of Agriculture scientist said Tuesday (May 22, 1990), showing that the global warming theory may be just a lot of hot air. 'On the average, the change at 961 official weather stations over the past 70 years was about a 0.33 degree decrease in average temperatures,' said Sherwood Idso, a physicist studying environmental change at the USDA's Agricultural Research Service at Phoenix...

"Idso said his study, which examined data between 1920 and 1984, showed hotter weather was linked more to population shifts. In areas where urbanization increased during the study period, temperatures tended to grow higher, he said.

"'Urban heat islands form when more people settle in an area' he said. 'Not only do they bring their own body heat, they burn fires, drive cars, and pave over land that used to reflect more heat and evaporate more water.'" (DA) About .05 degrees (10%) of the 0.5 degree Celsius increase in total average world temperature since 1881 has probably been caused by growth of cities. (IG6)

809 How do scientists measure past earth temperature during years before there were thermometers?

Scientists use historical records, tree rings, yearly ice layer thicknesses in ancient glaciers, and geological records such as the amount of Oxygen 18 in ocean floor cores to estimate ancient temperatures. (SY56)

810 How much has the earth warmed?

The amount the earth's temperature has changed depends on when one starts the measurement and when one stops. For example, i:

you measure the temperature change in your front yard, you will find a warming trend if you compare a typical April day to a cold winter day, but you will find a cooling trend if you compare the same April day to a hot summer day.

If we compare recent temperatures to those shortly after 1000 AD, we find that the earth is colder by about 0.5 to 2.0 degrees Celsius. However, the year used to begin most temperature comparisons is 1881, a colder than average year. Since 1881 was a colder than average year, of course, nearly all years since have been warmer. The average estimate is that the earth has warmed about 1/2 degree Celsius since the cold year of 1881. (It is more accurate to take an average of several years to prevent a warm or cool year from distorting a comparison. For example, taking 1987 and 1988 as the ending point would make it seem as if the earth had warmed nearly 0.5 degrees more than if 1992 and 1993 were taken as the end point). (RQ4, DV13)

811 Why is 1881 so frequently used as the first year for world temperature comparisons?

1881 is the first year when it is considered that temperatures were taken in enough places to make possible a reasonable estimate of average earth temperature.

812 Can the warming trend since the cold year 1881 be considered a return to normal?

Yes. 1881 was a very cold year, the increase since might be a return to normal. (DG6, DV10)

813 Could global warming have been slowed because the oceans have to absorb much energy before the land and air can warm?

No. The oceans are only slightly above freezing everywhere except near the surface. The surface water, 200 feet or less, floating on denser, colder, deep water, can be warmed by the sun. However, the surface water is not thick enough to store enough energy to slow any warming caused by other causes. (DV17) The inability of the oceans to substantially slow atmosphere warming is additionally proven by changes in only one year such as between 1991 and 1992 about equal to the 0.5 degree Celsius warming since 1881. (DV18)

814 What are the ways energy can be transmitted through our atmosphere?

Energy can be transmitted through our atmosphere in three ways, convection, conduction and radiation. Heat is a form of energy. Only radiation is changed by the greenhouse effect, and radiation from earth's surface is not the most important way for earth to eliminate energy.

Convection is the movement of a liquid or a gas. Earth's atmosphere is a gas and therefore transmits energy via convection. Convection is by far the most important way heat is transmitted from the earth's surface. Convection carries energy up above most of earth's atmosphere so that it can be radiated into outer space.

Conduction is energy transfer between the surfaces of two touching objects. An example of conduction is touching something hot with your finger. Conduction is the least important way heat is transmitted in earth's atmosphere.

Radiation is the transmission of energy via waves of the electromagnetic spectrum such as light, radio, etc. Radiation is the way energy from the sun is transmitted to earth's surface, the only way significant amounts of energy are transmitted to outer space from the top of earth's atmosphere, and the way a small percentage of the energy from earth's surface is transmitted to the top of the earth's atmosphere.

815 How does nature keep earth's average temperature about the same?

Radiation energy is measured in watts per square meter. The energy from a light bulb is about 100 watts. About 238 W/M^2 is absorbed by earth from solar radiation and a slight additional amount is generated on earth. All humans generate less than 1/10,000 as much energy as the 238 W/M^2 received from the sun. To keep earth's temperature about the same, about 238 W/M^2 must be radiated back to outer space. About 7% of the 238 W/M^2 is emitted from earth's surface through the atmosphere to outer space. The other 93% of the 238 W/M^2 is carried, usually by convection of water vapor, up to about four miles (6km) above earth's surface and above nearly all water vapor and most other greenhouse gases. From there the energy is radiated back into outer space.

816 What is the greenhouse effect?

The earth's atmosphere acts much like a greenhouse in that certain gases like the glass of a greenhouse let in sunlight and then trap outgoing radiation. The greenhouse effect in the earth's atmosphere for millions of years has made life possible by increasing the earth's temperature by about 33 degrees Celsius. (DV4, SY54) The concentration of some of these greenhouse gases in the atmosphere is increasing. The question is whether increasing greenhouse gases other than water will increase the already acting greenhouse effect and warm earth more than the present 33 degrees warming

817 Why do greenhouse gases absorb radiated energy from the earth and fail to absorb radiated energy from the sun?

All matter radiates and absorbs energy. The temperature of each radiating thing determines the amount, wavelength, energy and frequency of the radiation. The sun is hotter than the earth, so the sun's radiation is of higher energy and frequency than earth's radia tion. The wavelength of light is measured in microns, one-millionth of a meter, smaller than the width of a fine hair. Solar radiation averages about 1/2 micron (shorter wavelength means more energy) and earth radiation averages about 15 microns. Every gas best absorbs energy of certain wavelengths and frequencies. The earth's atmosphere in the absence of smoke and clouds is nearly transparent to energy from the sun but greenhouse gases absorb the less energetic, longer wavelength radiation from the earth.

818 What is the main greenhouse gas?

The main greenhouse gas (absorber of infrared radiation) in the atmosphere is water vapor, including clouds. Even if all other greenhouse gases (like carbon dioxide and methane) disappeared, we would still be left with over 98% of the current greenhouse effect. Carbon dioxide (CO_2) and all greenhouse gases other than water account for less than 2% of the greenhouse effect. (LI) Carbon dioxide is the second most important greenhouse gas, about twice as important as all other gases excluding water. Other major greenhouse gases include methane, nitrous oxide, ozone and freons, which together account for less than 1% of the greenhouse effect.

819 Why do increases of greenhouse gases have little effect on earth's temperature?

There are two main reasons why increased greenhouse gases in the atmosphere do not cause significant change in earth's temperature. First, water is such an efficient greenhouse energy absorber that where there is any significant amount of water vapor, the atmosphere already absorbs 100% of the energy radiated from the earth's surface and from the lower part of the earth's atmosphere. At any one time, about 93% of the energy from the earth's surface is absorbed by the atmosphere. More than 98% of this energy is absorbed by water in the air, even on clear days. The only places where substantial energy usually can be radiated directly from the earth's surface back into outer space are over deserts and cold polar regions. Deserts are dry and cold air holds very little water vapor, so cold polar regions have little water in the air, even on cloudy days.

Since the earth's greenhouse effect is already 93% effective, and much of the area where radiation can go directly from the surface to outer space is so cold that much less radiation occurs, how can earth radiate sufficient energy back to outer space to keep from being hotter?

Convection carries substantially all the energy from the earth's surface up about six kilometers (about four miles), above nearly all water vapor and above most greenhouse gases. From this height, energy can be radiated back into outer space with little interference from greenhouse gases.

87

A big part of the reason why additional greenhouse gases have so little effect on earth's temperature is that the outgoing energy is primarily emitted by water vapor from the top of the moist layer about 4 miles in altitude. Water vapor does not emit in the 7 to 10 micron region where most greenhouse gases absorb. Only CO_2 has a strong overlap with water vapor and in this overlap CO_2 absorption is already saturated.

820 Why is it important that carbon dioxide does not radiate to outer space from near earth's surface?

Satellite data shows that the radiation from carbon dioxide to outer space has a temperature of -50 to -55 degrees Celsius and therefore comes from about 12 to 20 km above earth's surface. This is at least twice as far above the level to which energy from earth's surface is carried by rising air currents (convection). From this it follows that a doubling or tripling of the amount of carbon dioxide in the atmosphere might raise the earth's temperature at 12 km above the surface, but would not substantially raise the temperature at or near earth's surface. (DV7)

821 Why is substantially all water vapor found in the lowest four miles in the earth's atmosphere in contrast to other gases which are spread uniformly, and why is that important?

Our atmosphere has many gases, but water is the only one that is a liquid at normal temperatures. Water's boiling point is 100 degrees Celsius, 212 degrees F. Even though water only boils at a hot temperature, some water evaporates at lower temperatures. The hotter the temperature, the more water can be held in air. At higher elevations in the atmosphere, the air is thinner and colder, so it is able to hold less water. Accordingly, nearly all water in the atmosphere is at lower altitudes where the air is warmer. This is important for greenhouse purposes, since convection carries energy about four miles high into the air, above most other greenhouse gases and nearly all water vapor, so increase of greenhouse gases within four miles of earth's surface will have little effect on radiation into outer space.

822 How much has CO_2 in the atmosphere increased?

CO_2 in the atmosphere increased from about 270 parts per million 200 years ago to about 350 parts per million (.035%) around 1990. (DV9, HD21)

823 How much is CO_2 projected to increase?

Some estimate that by 2050, CO_2 concentration will reach about .054%, about double the pre-industrial level of .027%. Others disagree, pointing out that since 1973, the rate of increase has apparently slowed, so that doubling will not occur before 2100. (LI)

824 Why do some scientists doubt that atmospheric CO_2 concentration will ever double?

Some point to the increase in plant and tree growth associated with the increase in carbon dioxide in the atmosphere and predict that carbon dioxide in the atmosphere is unlikely to ever double.

CO_2 is the major food of plants. When we calculate the amount of carbon that is burned, about 3 billion tons of carbon that theoretically should be added to atmospheric CO_2 disappear each year. What happens to this missing CO_2?

There are two major types of plants, C3 and C4. C3 plants are adapted to an atmosphere with much more CO_2, and increased CO_2 in the atmosphere makes C3 plants flourish. Thousands of experiments indicate that doubling atmospheric CO_2 concentration increases non-tree plant growth by about one-third. In addition, since the plants can take in CO_2 more quickly from an atmosphere richer in CO_2, the small pores in leaves through which CO_2 enters and through which water is lost need be open for a shorter time, thereby reducing water vapor loss by about a third, making it possible for plants to grow in dryer areas.

Tree growth increases with increased CO_2 even more than non-tree growth. Some young trees nearly triple their growth when growing in the presence of twice as much CO_2. An experiment with sour orange trees outside since 1988 in a plastic-wall environment where half the trees have an enriched CO_2 and half do not finds the CO_2 enriched trees growing nearly three times larger with about ten times more fruit. Increased tree growth has possibly removed the aforementioned 3 billion missing tons of CO_2 from the atmosphere each year. If true, this means that CO_2 will only increase by about 50% above present levels. If CO_2 increases by 50%, enhanced tree growth will apparently prevent any further increases in CO_2 by removing CO_2 as fast as additional carbon is burned.

It appears that modern trees grow and absorb CO_2 from the atmosphere about one-third faster than trees of 100 years ago when there was less CO_2 in the atmosphere. (ID)

825 Do people produce other air pollution that tends to cool the earth?

Yes. Particulates and sulfur dioxide, for example, increase the amount of solar energy reflected back into space before it can warm the earth. This may be part of the reason why the northern hemisphere, where most air pollution is generated, shows no net warming during the past half century. (WI)

826 Do volcanic eruptions change the temperature of the atmosphere?

Yes, if they are large enough. Cold years have frequently followed large volcanic eruptions. 1992 and 1993 followed a large volcanic eruption and were nearly 0.5 degrees cooler than 1990 and 1991. The stratosphere after the 1991 Mt Pinatubo eruption became colder than any time in at least 15 and possibly more than 40 years.(CW3) In contrast, 1987-1990, with less volcanic activity, were very warm.

827 What is the basis for allegations that global warming will exceed one degree Celsius?

People who developed computer models without enough accurate information about atmospheric thermodynamics are the main source of beliefs of great atmospheric warming.

828 How can we be certain that the computer models predicting greater atmospheric warming are incorrect?

The computer models fail every significant test of their accuracy as follows:

1) If they were correct, since we have already had a 50% increase in carbon dioxide, we should have already had about three times as much warming as has occurred.

2) Nearly all atmospheric warming since 1881 took place before 1940, but nearly all the increase in carbon dioxide has occurred since 1940.

3) The computer models contain incorrect information.

4) The computer models lack information necessary for understanding how the earth's atmosphere works.

5) The atmosphere's temperature has not increased at the rate, in the amount, or at the locations that it had to increase according to any of the computer models.

6) All the computer models grossly simplify the atmosphere, rather than calculating based on a reasonable description of atmospheric complexity.

7) Computer models have made errors of more than eight degrees Celsius in predicting current atmospheric temperatures in certain areas. This is a great mistake when one considers that the difference in earth temperature between the coldest and warmest year is only about one degree Celsius.

8) Computer models do not properly calculate that substantially all energy radiated to outer space is first carried up to about four miles above the earth's surface by rising air currents.

9) Computer models do not properly calculate that substantially all energy radiated to outer space is first used to evaporate water then carried above about four miles, then released by conversion of water vapor to rain. (DV, HD39)

829 What is the difference in average world temperature between the coldest and warmest years since 1881?

About one degree Celsius. (DV9)

830 What energy is trapped by the greenhouse effect?

Radiated energy from the earth's surface.

831 Did most of the warming since 1881 occur before the greenhouse effect could have caused it?

Yes. The times around 1920 and 1940 were warm and this warming occurred before there was enough CO_2 in the atmosphere to have caused it. There was cooling in the years before 1980 during a time of great increase in CO_2.

832 What is wrong with the predicted pattern of global warming?

1) The beginning years were so cold that the present might just be a return to normal temperatures

2) Nearly all warming took place before there was enough CO_2 increase to have caused it.

3) Any greenhouse warming would include a pattern of warming over land and sea, over certain latitudes (distance from the equator), and at certain altitudes (distance from the ground). The observed pattern of warming fails these necessary tests and must have some cause other than increased greenhouse effect. (DV)

833 What has apparently caused the 0.5 degree Celsius increase in temperature since 1881?

Perhaps the best explanation of differences in average earth temperature is change in solar activity. "All the significant changes in global temperature in the last 100 years faithfully track the changes in solar surface activity. The agreement is too close to be readily dismissed as coincidence." (GW16,17) "Baliunal, et al. have combined observations of the sun and solar-type stars to obtain the relationship between solar luminosity and changes in the sun's surface magnetic activity. Their results indicate that the marked increase in solar surface activity recorded in the last 100 years corresponds to a brightening of the sun by 0.7%, in good agreement with the estimated change in solar brightness needed to explain the recent global warming." (GW18,19) "A comparison between the carbon-14 record and the record of ancient climates, obtained from geologic evidence of the advance and retreat of glaciers, reveals that all but one of the major decreases in solar activity in the last 1000 years were accompanied by cold spells in the climate record." (GW19) Other scientists have criticized the preceding analysis, claiming that the effect of solar variability will be less than claimed by Baliunal.

Professor Robert Balling of Arizona State University has estimated that 50% of global warming since 1881 can be accounted for by changes related neither to CO_2 nor to solar activity. He states, for example, that a reduction in volcanic activity accounts for 30% of the observed warming. (IG6)

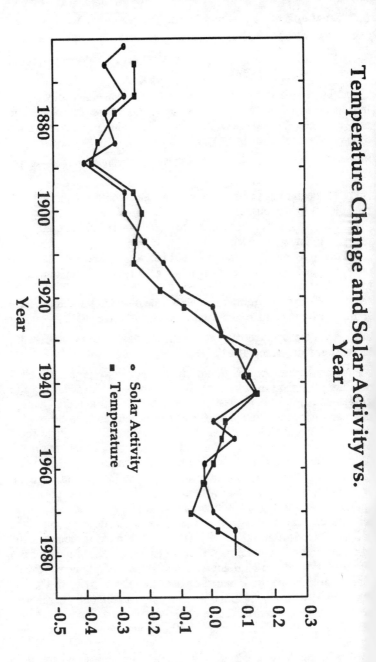

Temperature Change and Solar Activity vs. Year

- Solar Activity
- Temperature

Year

Temperature Anomaly (°C)

92

REFERENCES

The term "Cato" in the following footnotes refers to papers prepared for the Cato Institute conference on "Global Environmental Crises: Science or Politics?" Washingon DC, June 5-6, 1991

(CW) *Climate Watch,* The Bulletin of the Global Climate Coalition, Vol 1, Issue 10, October, 1993.

(DA) 1990 US Department of Agriculture (Phoenix) 70 year study of US temperature data, released May 22, 1990, and carried by AP wire, published Orange County Register, May 23, 1990

(DG) Andrew R. Solow of Woods Hole Oceanographic Institute, *The Detection of Greenhouse Warming,* (Cato)

(DV) Hugh Ellsaesser, *A Different View of the Climatic Effects of CO_2—Updated,* accepted by Lawrence Livermore National Laboratory 8/31/89 for the US Department of Energy, Atmospheric and Climatic Research Div., under contract W-7405-ENG-48

(GW) Robert Jastrow, et al., *Global Warming Update,* (1992) George Marshall Institute

(HD) Robert C. Balling, director of the office of Climatology, Arizona State Univ., *The Heated Debate,* Pacific Research Institute for Public Policy (1992)

(ID) *Carbon Dioxide and Global Change,* Sherwood Idso, IBR Press

(IG) Robert C. Balling, Jr., Office of Climatology, Arizona State University, *Interpreting the Global Temperature Effect,* (Cato)

(LI) Personal communication from Hugh Ellsaesser guest scientist at Lawrence Livermore National Laboratory

(ON) Richard S. Lindzen, Massachusetts Institute of Technology, *Global Warming: The Origin and Nature of Alleged Scientific Consensus,* (Cato)

(PS) Patrick J. Michaels, Dept. of Environmental Sciences, Univ. of Virginia, *The Political Science of Global Warming,* (Cato)

(RQ) Richard S. Lindzen, Alfred P. Sloan Professor of Meterology, Massachusetts Institute of Technology, *Reasons for Questioning Global Warming Predictions,* (Cato)

(SC) Friis-Christensen, E and K Lassen, <u>Science</u> 254, 698 (1991) cited also in *Global Warming Update* George Marshal Institute (1992) Washington, DC

(SP) Robert Jastrow, et al., *Scientific Perspectives on the Greenhouse Problem,* Marshal Press (1990)

(SY) Hugh W. Ellsaesser, *Setting the 10,000-Year Climate Record Straight,* Winter 1991 21st Century p.52

(WI) Wigley, T.M.L., 1989. "Possible Climate Change due to SO2-Derived Cloud Condensation Nuclei". *Nature* 338, 365-367.

CHAPTER 9

OZONE

901 What is ozone?
902 What is ultraviolet radiation?
903 What is the ozone hole threat theory?
904 What do population control advocates say about ozone?
905 What do those who deny that ozone is a serious problem allege?
906 What do atmosphere specialists say about ozone?
907 How do atmospheric ozone concentrations vary?
908 How have estimates of ozone depletion changed?
909 Do calculations of ozone depletion consider chlorine from nature?
910 What are the different types of ultraviolet radiation?
911 What does ultraviolet C radiation do?
912 Why is ozone necessary to stop ultraviolet B radiation?
913 How does the atmosphere self-correct to protect us from greater amounts of ultraviolet B radiation?
914 How much does the average amount of ultraviolet B radiation reaching an area depend on distance from the equator?
915 Why can people live at the equator if the equator receives so much more ultraviolet B radiation than polar regions?
916 Has it been proven that freon-like gases destroy substantial amounts of ozone in the atmosphere?
917 What is the scientific basis for the belief that freons destroy the earth's ozone layer?
918 Is there evidence from nature that freon molecules are not numerous enough to be a threat to ozone?
919 How long does ozone last in the atmosphere?
920 Does one volcano release most of the chlorine into the Antarctic atmosphere?
921 How old is the Antarctic ozone hole?
922 Why is there an ozone hole in Antarctica, rather than farther north where nearly all the freons are released to the atmosphere?
923 Have large volcanic eruptions been followed by a decrease in atmosphere ozone?

901 What is ozone?

Ozone is a form of oxygen. Normal oxygen has two atoms and is called O_2. O_2 is very stable and hard to break apart. Ozone has three atoms. Called O_3, ozone is less stable and easier to break apart than O_2. In fact, laboratory tests have indicated that chlorine can break apart ozone. When close to the ground, ozone is one of the major elements of smog, but high in the air ozone absorbs harmful ultraviolet radiation.

902 What is ultraviolet radiation?

Ultraviolet radiation or rays such as those received from the sun are electro-magnetic waves similar to visible light, but shorter in wavelength and higher in both frequency and energy than visible light.

903 What is the ozone hole threat theory?

Ozone high in the atmosphere absorbs ultraviolet B radiation. The ozone hole threat theory alleges that:

a) By releasing chlorine into the atmosphere, we will destroy much of the ozone in the upper atmosphere;

b) Less ozone means more ultraviolet B radiation reaches the earth's surface; and

c) More ultraviolet B radiation will cause more sunburn and associated damage such as skin cancer.

904 What do population control advocates say about ozone?

Population control advocates say that:

a) The ozone high above the ground is being destroyed by chlorine released from freon-like compounds used in appliances such as refrigerators and air conditioners.

b) This freon destruction theory has been proven.

c) There is no natural explanation for the ozone hole.

d) Destruction of ozone has caused the amount of ultraviolet B radiation received at the earth's surface to increase.

e) The ozone hole is new and did not exist before freons were developed.

f) Thousands, perhaps millions of people will die from skin cancer caused by ozone destruction.

g) The ozone hole is growing, and ozone destruction will cause holes over the US.

905 What do those who deny that ozone is a serious problem allege?

Those who deny that loss of upper atmospheric ozone is a serious problem allege:

a) The belief that freon-like compounds destroy significant amounts of ozone high in the atmosphere is an unproven theory.

b) The freon destruction of ozone theory has not been proven. The vast majority of the evidence indicates that freon does not substantially lower the amount of ozone in the upper atmosphere. In fact, ozone seems more sensitive to temperature, water vapor, sulfuric and nitric acid (from volcanoes), and particles than to chlorine.

c) There has been no slow steady progression in the depth and size of the ozone hole as the amount of freon and chlorine in the atmosphere has increased, as one would expect if freons were destroying chlorine. One natural explanation is that the ozone hole is ephemeral and comes and goes as a function of changes in temperature, water vapor, particles and sulfuric and nitric acid.

d) Ultraviolet B radiation at the earth's surface has fequently decreased as ozone decreased, possibly because both decrease when the sun is less active.

e) We do not know that the ozone hole is new.

f) The type of skin cancer usually caused by ultraviolet B radiation is not the deadly type which is called melanoma but is usually benign cancer which seldom kills. Melanoma frequently occurs in covered areas of the body which are not exposed to the sun.

Sunburn and excess exposure to the sun cause harm, but increased ultraviolet radiation is associated with a decrease in total cancer deaths, since the increased ultraviolet radiation helps prevent other cancers.

g) The ozone hole will change in size with differences in conditions, but it is unlikely to grow substantially because no other place is both isolated from winds and has the winter darkness of the Antarctic winter. Only a 3% reduction over the US was predicted by the original theory. Under the ozone hole in Antarctica, much less ultraviolet radiation is received than at the equator. (EL)(HH8)

906 What do atmosphere specialists say about ozone?

As in the case of global warming, there is a split with those having the best direct understanding of how the atmosphere works claiming that the ozone scare is nonsense. Those who allege that the ozone threat is immediate, very serious, and requires drastic action are more likely to deal only indirectly with the atmosphere.

907 How do atmospheric ozone concentrations vary?

There is an 11 year solar radiation cycle which causes an 11 year cycle in atmospheric ozone concentration, and different solar cycles are not identical. Polar winters are dark, and sunlight is necessary for ozone formation. Ozone has seasonal swings of 10% to 50% within a few weeks. Accordingly, whether ozone increases or decreases depends on the starting date and ending date compared.

908 How have estimates of ozone depletion changed?

"National Academy of Sciences in 1979 calculated an 18% ozone depletion due to CFCs (freons), a 9% effect in 1982, but only a 3% effect in their 1984 report." (SO1)

909 Do calculations of ozone depletion consider chlorine from nature?

No. "A major criticism of the calculations is that they do not consider the input of chlorine and bromine from natural sources..."(SO1)

910 What are the different types of ultraviolet radiation?

It is convenient to divide ultraviolet radiation from the sun or other sources into three energy levels: ultraviolet C, most energetic and highest in frequency; B, intermediate in energy; and A, least energetic and lowest in frequency. Ultraviolet A is closest in wavelength, frequency and energy to visible light. Ultraviolet B is the radiation that causes sunburn and skin cancer.

911 What does ultraviolet C radiation do?

Ultraviolet C, which is absorbed by regular oxygen (about 20% of the atmosphere), makes ozone. Because it is easily absorbed, ultraviolet C reaches the earth's surface only in negligible amounts. In the upper atmosphere, ultraviolet C hits oxygen (O_2) molecules, giving up energy which splits O_2 into two oxygen atoms (O_1). Each O_1 immediately recombines with another O_1 to form another oxygen molecule O_2 or combines with an O_2 to form O_3 which is ozone. By this process, billions of tons of O_3 are formed every second in the daylight atmosphere.

912 Why is ozone necessary to stop ultraviolet B radiation?

Ozone is the gas in the atmosphere most effective in stopping ultraviolet B radiation. Ozone is only a tiny percentage of the atmosphere, far less than 1%. If the amount of ozone is reduced, less ultraviolet B will be absorbed by the atmosphere.

913 How does the atmosphere self-correct to protect us from greater amounts of ultraviolet B radiation?

When the sun radiates more intensely, more ultraviolet B radiation reaches the earth. The more intense sunlight includes more ultraviolet C radiation. The additional ultraviolet C radiation makes more ozone which absorbs more ultraviolet B radiation. Similarly, lower ozone levels caused by less ultraviolet C radiation have been associated with less ultraviolet B radiation reaching earth since less is transmitted to the earth.

914 How much does the average amount of ultraviolet B radiation reaching an area depend on distance from the equator?

The amount of ultraviolet B radiation reaching an area depends on latitude. There is a steady increase as one approaches lower latitudes (moves from pole toward the equator). The equator receives about 50 times as much as regions around the north and south poles. This is because equatorial sunlight comes at a steeper angle and has less atmosphere to pass through before reaching the earth's surface near the equator. In addition, the sun does not rise far above the horizon at the poles, so because of the more shallow angle, the same amount of sunlight is divided over a greater area nearer the poles. At latitudes such as those of the US, moving 600 miles south doubles the amount of ultraviolet B radiation reaching earth's surface. Moving six miles south increases the amount of ultraviolet B by about 1%.

If the worst predicted destruction of ozone actually occurs, the increase in ultraviolet B radiation will be the equivalent to moving from the north end to the south end of a large metropolitan area. An increase of a few percent at the pole or at middle latitudes would not bring the intensity of ultraviolet B radiation received there to even a large fraction of present amounts received at the equator. The present amount received at the equator is not a serious health risk.

915 Why can people live at the equator if the equator receives so much more ultraviolet B radiation than polar regions?

First, most ultraviolet B radiation never reaches the earth's surface. Since the equator's high atmosphere receives more ultraviolet B radiation that harms humans, it must also receive more ultraviolet C radiation. More ultraviolet C radiation makes far more high atmosphere ozone above the equator than above the poles. The ozone absorbs vast amounts of ultraviolet B radiation in the high atmosphere, reducing the amount that penetrates down to the earth's surface. In addition, the amount of ultraviolet B radiation received at the poles is so small that the increased amount, 50 times as much, received at the equator is not a serious health risk. Since ultraviolet B actually seems to prevent other cancers apparently by increasing the amount of Vitamin D produced by the skin, the overall chance of cancer death is not greater among people living near the equator. (HO8)

916 Has it been proven that freon-like gases destroy substantial amounts of ozone in the atmosphere?

No. In fact there are good reasons to doubt that freon-like gases substantially affect the ozone layer:

a) Freon-like gases have been shown to destroy ozone under laboratory conditions, but not in the actual atmosphere where, admittedly, such proof would be difficult. It is thought that the freon breaks up releasing chlorine, and each chlorine atom then breaks up many thousands of ozone molecules.

b) Substantial amounts of freon necessary to affect the ozone layer cannot be found in the region more than twenty miles above the earth where the ozone layer exists. Only about 7500 tons of freon is believed to be high enough in the atmosphere to destroy ozone, not enough to substantially affect the billions of tons of ozone formed every second.

917 What is the scientific basis for the belief that freons destroy the earth's ozone layer?

The most common freons or CFCs are CFC-11 and CFC-12. The chemical formula for CFC-12 is CCl_2F_2. The proposed chemical reaction is CCl_2F_2 plus ultraviolet radiation = $CClF_2$+ plus Cl-. The single chlorine atom then attacks an ozone (O_3) molecule. Cl- + O_3 yields ClO- + O_2. In theory, the ClO then reacts with oxygen to once again release the Cl-. Rowland and Molina formulated this theory in a laboratory. It has not been tested in the high atmosphere. They claim that a single Cl- ion can destroy hundreds of thousands of ozone molecules via a series of reactions.

918 Is there evidence from nature that freon molecules are not numerous enough to be a threat to ozone?

Freon is stable in the low atmosphere. The freon destroying ozone theory alleges that of about 1,000,000 tons of CFCs produced annually, about 7,500 tons reaches the high atmosphere where it is broken up by ultraviolet radiation, releasing Cl- which destroys ozone. Solar radiation includes ultraviolet C which makes billions of tons of ozone per second in the atmosphere. There are 3600 seconds in an hour, 86,400 in a day and about 31 million in a year, so the sun makes 31 million times billions of tons of ozone every year. That 7,500 tons of freons would have to work very hard and move around very fast to have a substantial effect on the ozone, since there are trillions of tons of ozone made each year for every ton of chlorine released in the high atmosphere each year. It has been claimed that a single chlorine atom may destroy as many as 100,000 molecules of ozone, but even if that is true, that would be far less than necessary to make an ozone hole. Nobody has shown how the chlorine ions formed by 7,500 tons of freon could move fast enough and accurately enough to cause chemical reactions having a significant effect on the billions of tons of ozone formed and destroyed by ultraviolet light each second in the upper atmosphere.

919 How long does ozone last in the atmosphere?

How long the ozone lasts after it is formed depends on the amount of ultraviolet radiation to which it is exposed. While ultraviolet C creates ozone, ultraviolet B destroys it. When ultraviolet C and B are present in large amounts, ozone is created in large amounts but destroyed quickly. Since ultraviolet is absorbed by the atmosphere, the amount of ultraviolet radiation and thus the length of ozone's life is dependent on altitude. In the lower atmosphere, about half the ozone created at any given time is destroyed after days or months. In the upper atmosphere, half the ozone is destroyed after minutes or seconds. Chlorine is not necessary to explain the destruction of atmospheric ozone. If chlorine destroyed substantial amounts of atmosphere ozone, the half life of ozone might not be so much greater at low altitudes.

920 Does one volcano release most of the chlorine into the Antarctic atmosphere?

Mt. Erebus, a volcano in Antarctica, annually and fairly regularly releases into the lower Antarctic atmosphere about 365,000 tons of chlorine (HO p14 quoting 1983 observations of volcanologist William Rose published in *Nature Magazine*). Mt Erebus does not send much of this chlorine into the upper atmosphere, since its eruptions are not ordinarily explosive. This observation has been criticized.

921 How old is the Antarctic ozone hole?

We do not know.

922 Why is there an ozone hole in Antarctica, rather than farther north where nearly all the freons are released to the atmosphere?

Antarctica has darkness during nearly half the year. In these Antarctic winter months there is no sunlight to make new ozone. Additionally, Antarctic wind patterns are such that little ozone formed elsewhere is carried to the Antarctic during this dark time. During the Antarctic winter there is little sunlight to form new ozone. About September, at the end of winter, seasonal conditions cause the hole to form. The hole usually breaks up during November when the spring wind pattern first forms. The Arctic also has a dark winter, but its different wind patterns bring in ozone formed where there still is sunlight and prevent formation of an ozone hole.

923 Have large volcanic eruptions been followed by a decrease in atmosphere ozone?

Yes. Large volcanic eruptions, such as Mt. Pinatubo in 1991, were followed by decreases in atmosphere ozone concentration lasting several years. (EL)

REFERENCES

(EL)   data from Hugh Ellsaesser atmosphere guest scientist at University of California Lawrence Livermore Laboratory
(HH)   Hugh Ellsaesser, guest scientist at Lawrence Livermore National Laboratory Livermore, CA, *The Holes in the Ozone Hole, I and II*
(HO)   Rogelio Maduro and Ralf Schaurhammer, *The Holes in the Ozone Scare*, 21st Century Science Associates, Washington DC 1992
(IA)   International Association for meteorology and Atmosphere Physics, International Ozone Commission, WORKSHOP ON INTERNATIONAL OZONE August 4-6 preceding Quadrennial Ozone Symposium, August 8-13, 1988 U of Gottingen, Germany
(SO)   S. Fred Singer, *Stratospheric Ozone: Science and Policy* paper

CHAPTER 10

QUALITY OF LIFE

1001 What is quality of life?

Quality of life means different things to different people. To the extremely wealthy, it may mean better servants, or a larger yacht. To some others, it may mean travel, great museums and art, good operas, a beautiful or empty beach or wilderness, or something else entirely.

To the average person in the world though, it has more practical meanings and quality of life is measured by the following 20 things listed by UNICEF in the following order: under 5 mortality rate, infant mortality rate, gross national product per capita, life expectancy, adult literacy, % children in school, % infants with low birth weight, % children under weight or stunted, rate of improvement of food supply, daily per capita calorie supply, % of household income spent on food and cereals, % with access to safe water, adequate sanitation and health services, % immunized, availability of oral rehydration therapy, radio and TV sets, school enrollment, death rate, growth of gross national product per capita, and % below absolute poverty level. (SW68-85)

The *UN Statistical Yearbook* lists the conditions of the following to indicate quality of life: food, industrial production, commodities production, mining, manufacturing, motor vehicle production and use, trade, minerals, electricity use, light industry, heavy industry, paper, chemicals, metals and metal products, textiles, productivity in about 20 different areas, energy supply and consumption, education, literacy, life expectancy, infant mortality, child mortality, maternal mortality, and TV and radio receivers. (SYv)

1002 What do the measures of quality of life listed by UNICEF and the UN Statistical Yearbook show?

As world population has increased, each and every one of the more than 40 measures of quality of life has improved. Each and

101

every one of the more than 40 measures of quality of life is better on average both in more densely populated countries and also in more densely populated parts of individual countries.

1003   What does the most important measure of quality of life show?

The most important measure of quality of life is life expectancy, because improvements in other areas related to quality of life also increase life expectancy. Life expectancy in the developing countries increased from 46 years to 61 years between 1960 and 1991 during the time of the so-called population explosion. (DYv) (SW76, 77)

1004   What does United Nations data show about changes in economic quality of life for the average person in the world?

During the most recent time of fast population growth after 1948, quality of life has improved faster than ever before in world history. During the recent slowing in population growth since about 1970 in developed countries, the rate of improvement has continued, but has slowed. By every one of more than 40 amenities measured, the quality of life is improving very quickly. Americans often take things like good housing, sufficient food, electricity, good water, telephones, radios, refrigerators, TVs, etc. for granted. In most areas of the world, until recently, only the wealthy owned these signs of a good modern life. Now the number of households owning these signs of middle class American life is increasing far faster than population is growing. In each recent period of 10 years, world population has increased by about 20%. During the same 10 years, the number of telephones, radios, refrigerators, TVs and many other amenities in use approximately doubled. If recent trends continue, by the year 2,000 most of the homes of the world will have most of the major amenities that have improved American life during the 20th Century. (SYv) (SW68-85)

UNICEF summarizes as follows: "Since the end of the Second World War, average real incomes in the developing world have more than doubled; infant and child death rates have been more than halved; average life expectancy has increased by about a third; the proportion of the developing world's children starting school has risen to more than three-quarters; and the percentage of rural families with access to safe water has increased from 10% to almost 60%." (SW Preface)

1005   What is the best way to decide if one area has a better quality of life than another area?

Determine which areas people are moving from and which areas people are moving to.

Under-5 Deaths by Main Cause, Developing Countries, 1990

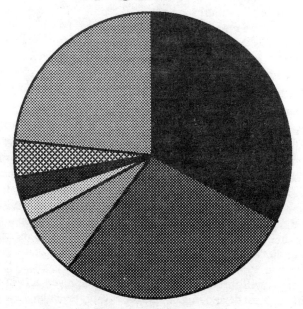

Total: 12.9 million deaths

- Pneumonia 27.9%
- Measle 6.8%
- Whooping 2.8%
- Tuberculosis 2.3%
- Neonatal 4.3%
- Diarrhoeal 23.3%
- Other 32.6%

1006 What does immigration tell us about population density and the quality of life?

The primary immigration of the world has been from less crowded areas to more crowded areas, from rural areas to urban areas. This has been true during nearly all times in nearly all countries. In developed countries, this has led to a growth of suburbs where middle class people have been able to own more land and have bigger houses. The suburbs are not an exception to the general rule, since they are the outlying part of a city and are far more crowded than rural areas. Nearly everywhere, people have been voting with their feet for a higher quality of life by moving to more densely populated urban areas.

1007 Has improvement in productivity improved quality of life?

Productivity continues to increase in every way measured. From 1980 to 1989, world industrial productivity improved by 41%, far faster than population grew. (SY92 p 34) From 1980 to 1989, in developing countries, productivity grew as follows: total productivity grew 50%, heavy industry grew 77%, total manufacturing grew 50%, and textiles grew 61%. (SY92 p 38) During the time of fast population growth since 1948, for the first time in world history, the situation of nearly everyone on earth has vastly improved. In developing countries where most of the people live, education spending adjusted for inflation became at least five times greater from 1975 to 1989. (SY92 pp 127-134) This vast increase in educated people will further accelerate the vast improvements in quality of life in most developing countries. The improvements in manufacturing productivity have made possible the more than doubling of real income which has reduced problems caused by poverty.

REFERENCES

(DY) *United Nations Demographic Yearbook*, published annually.
(SW) United Nations Children's Fund (UNICEF), *THE STATE OF THE WORLD'S CHILDREN 1993*, published by Oxford University Press
(SY) *United Nations Statistical Yearbook*, published annually.
(v)   indicates the data is available by comparing various years.

CHAPTER 11

WHY WE SHOULD GROW

1101 Why should we prefer a young, growing population to an old stagnant one?

1102 How much do increases in population density increase productivity?

1103 Has population stagnation or decline ever had a positive result?

1104 How does population growth benefit a people?

1105 What is the ratio of the cost to society of people over the age of 65 to people under the age of 18?

1106 What is the evidence that population growth generally improves quality of life?

1101 Why should we prefer a young, growing population to an old stagnant one?

Original thinking and enthusiasm for new ideas are far more likely to come from the young than the aged. Little great art, few great books, practically no great music, few plays worth mentioning, practically no great ideas, inventions or scientific theories, and practically no great philosophies have come from elderly people. Old populations are more rigid in their ways. They become more security conscious and far less progressive. Accordingly, progress in countries with old populations is likely to slow or stop.

In a similar manner, when population growth stops, there is no need to build new buildings, to devise new ideas, and to do other things characteristic of vigorous societies.

The tendency for population growth to force benefits on a nation which is growing has been analyzed in detail by Colin Clark (PG), as well as by Sauvy (TG) and many historians. The reader in doubt should consult Clark or Sauvy or correlate population increase or stagnation in each country at each time with the positive characteristics of the nations at that time.

1102 How much do increases in population density increase productivity?

Increases in population density increase productivity by the one-sixth power of the increase. For a rigorous proof and details, see (PG261).

1103 Has population stagnation or decline ever had a happy result?

No. Sauvy examines history and comes to this conclusion (TG Vol. 2 p 10).

1104 How does population growth benefit a people?

Certain things are necessary for what is now considered civilized living. A more dense population can provide these things at a much lower cost per person. There are costs which occur when large numbers of people live relatively close together, such as in cities, but these costs are far more than offset by the benefits which result from the higher population. Examples of this include development of ports, airports, highways and railroads. The cost is about the same regardless of the population, but the cost per person depends on the number of people. The more people, the less cost per person. This question and answer are analyzed in detail by Colin Clark (PG256-277).

A second major benefit comprises lower prices of items that must be transported and distributed to consumers. A simple test of this principle would be to compare gasoline prices, or the prices of similar items in city and rural areas.

1105   What is the ratio of the cost to society of people over the age of 65 to people under the age of 18?

The young and the old are usually non-workers. Parents support their children. There is a cost for the raising of each child. Elderly people are supported by Social Security, their relatives, their savings, etc. The expense necessary to maintain an elderly person is substantially higher than the cost for a younger person, because older persons have more expensive needs such as medical care. On the average, the cost to maintain an old person at a middle class standard of living is about 3 to 4 times as great as the cost to maintain a person who is under the age of 14.

Accordingly, although older people are valuable for non-economic reasons, economically, a younger society spends a lesser percentage of total income supporting its non-working members.

1106   What is the evidence that population growth generally improves quality of life?

For more details, please see Chapter 10. There are at least 9 ways to test this question, and each test indicates that population growth in most cases will improve the quality of life.

1) In all of human history, there has been only one time of rapid prolonged world population increase. That is the one that started about 1945. There has been only one time when the quality of life of the average person has substantially improved, and it occurred during the same time since 1945 when population grew fastest. This has also been the only time when the diet and the life expectancy of the average person has substantially improved. So, this first test shows that population growth has been associated with improving, not hurting the quality of life.

2) During human history, have those nations which have had a stagnant or declining population growth rate on average prospered? No. Thousands of nations and communities have existed during human history. Sauvy was asked by the French government after

the Second World War to study history to find out what effects population growth or stagnation had on nations. Sauvy studied all of human history for the French Government and could not find even one example of population decline or population stagnation which had a positive result. (TG) So by the second test, it appears that population growth is better.

3) Are the wealthy nations of the world and those nations with a high quality of life more or less crowded than average? If the population control arguments are correct, we would expect these nations to be relatively empty. Just the opposite is true. Many nations having a high quality of life are 10 times or even more crowded than the world average.

4) Compare the population densities of developed countries and developing countries. If population control is the answer to the world's problems, we would expect the underdeveloped countries to be far more crowded than the most crowded developed countries. Just the opposite is true. The developed countries in the world are on average more densely populated. In fact, some US states are nearly twice as crowded as countries like India and China.

5) Is the quality of life better in the more or the less densely populated areas within individual nations? Here, again, by most tests and in most areas, the quality of life is far higher in more crowded areas within countries.

6) Are the people of the world moving toward areas of less population density or more population density? This is a vote by people's feet. You could expect them to move toward a place where there is a higher quality of life. Here again the answer is that most people are moving to more densely populated countries and to more densely populated areas within countries, indicating that the quality of life is greater in more crowded areas. (SYv) (SW76,77)

7) Examine those nations which were poor a generation ago and ask whether the quality of life has improved more or less depending on whether the population has grown more or less? Population control flunks the test. Those nations with fast population growth have been improving their quality of life and standard of living far faster than those nations with slower population growth. (SW68-85) (SYv)

8) The birth rate dropped very fast during the past generation in both developing and developed countries. The birth rate dropped earlier and far below replacement level in Europe, slightly below replacement level in the rest of the developed world and dropped toward replacement level in the developing countries. The birth rate drop has been followed a generation later (when fewer young people enter the labor force because fewer were previously born) by a lingering economic sickness that is about proportional to the drop in birth rate.

107

9) Do a higher percentage of the people live in urban areas in developed or developing countries? UNICEF ranks 129 countries into four groups according to under five mortality, which correlates well with quality of life. The least developed countries are 26% urbanized. The second worst problems are found in a group that is 40% urbanized. The middle group are 56% urbanized. The most developed group are 73% urbanized. None of the countries in the least developed is as urbanized as the average of the most developed group and all of the countries of the most developed group are more urbanized than the average of the least developed group. (SW76,77)

REFERENCES

(PG)   Colin Clark, *Population Growth and Land Use*
(SW)   United Nation's Children's Fund (UNICEF), *THE STATE OF THE WORLD'S CHILDREN 1993*, Oxford University Press
(SYv) *UN Statistical Yearbook*, published annually, compare data in various years
(TG)   Alfred Sauvy, *Theoria Generale De La Population*

CHAPTER 12

COMPUTERS

1201 What is a computer?
1202 Are computers any more likely to tell the truth than pencils, pens or word processors?
1203 What are the advantages of using a computer if one intends to lie?
1204 How accurate have major population studies aided by computers been?

1201 What is a computer?

A computer is an electronic information storage and processing machine. As computers become more advanced, efficient and effective, they do more that we consider to be thinking. A good way to consider a computer is to think of it as a pencil that permits the user to write and calculate extremely fast.

1202 Are computers any more likely to tell the truth than pencils, pens or word processors?

Computers are as likely, but no more likely to tell the truth than pencils, pens or word processors. In each case, the likelihood for truth depends on the information the user enters into the computer. A liar is just as capable of lying using a computer as using a pen, pencil or word processor.

1203 What are the advantages of using a computer if one intends to lie?

The calculations done by a computer are so complex and voluminous and the methods used to set them up can be so obscure that some people will accept calculations rather than try to double-check them. The computer data is electronically stored in the computer, and one cannot access and check it unless one obtains the permission of the person controlling the computer. If the computer was used to lie, this permission may not be given. Most people do not understand computers and assume that if data was processed by computer, the result is probably better than a guess or a lie. There is a natural assumption that if anyone cared enough to go to the trouble of using a computer, they were careful enough to use correct information and program a correct method of performing the calculations.

1204 How accurate have major population studies aided by computers been?

They have all been nothing more than methods of publicizing false information. No useful or valid information was generated by any of them.

The first major population study aided by computer was by the 1970 Presidential Commission, chaired by John D. Rockefeller and entitled *Population Growth and the American Future*. In 1952, Rockefeller had founded the first population control organization, the Population Council. As one might expect, most of the other commissioners had previous associations with population control organizations. The report received massive publicity, even though it came to false conclusions based on false information and erroneous calculations.

The second major population study by computer was *The Limits to Growth: A Report for the Club of Rome's Project on the Predicament of Mankind* D.H. Meadows et al., Universe Books, NY (1972). The man who headed the sponsoring Club of Rome and controlled those who authored *Limits to Growth*, Italian industrialist Aurelio Peccei, admitted that *Limits* was intended to jolt people and further admitted that false information was intentionally placed in <u>Limits</u> to make it more effective propaganda. (TI)

The third major population study by computer was the *Global 2000 Report to the President* (1980) by the Carter Administration. For a detailed analysis, please see *Response to the Global 2000 Report* by Julian Simon and Herman Kahn. Comparing the response to the report shows that those in control of the report used false information and calculated incorrectly. For example, *Global 2000* predicted that 500,000 species would become extinct between 1980 and 2000. In the face of this, the U.S. government has only confirmed that 7 species became extinct between 1973 and 1993. (FW)

REFERENCES

(FW)   Telephone call to U.S. Department of Interior Fish and Wild Life, (202)343-5634
(TI)   *Time* magazine, Apr 26, 1976, p 56

Play population trivia with these TRUE/FALSE questions
Answers follow with references.

CHAPTER 1—UNDERSTANDING POPULATION

1. The earth could support an infinite number of people.
2. The population controversy is whether or not there are going to be too many people
3. Population control involves governments forcing people to have fewer children.
4. Traditional Christianity orders us to not multiply and not fill the earth.
5. The U.S. Government Global 2000 report predicted $3 per gallon gasoline.
6. Predictions of population control advocates have usually been correct.
7. Population control advocates claim that a lack of petroleum is the most important reason for limiting population.
8. UNICEF claims that 40,000 children die daily from malnutrition.
9. More than 70% of child deaths are in countries where the average number of calories consumed exceeds the U.S. recommendation.
10. The World Bank claims that 13% of children are malnourished in a country with greater calorie consumption than Canada.
11. The World Bank claims that in a country with a life expectancy greater than 70, 45% of children are malnourished.

CHAPTER 2—FOOD

12. Starvation is more likely in large population countries.
13. High average population density is associated with more starvation.
14. Less food grown per person is the leading cause of malnutrition related deaths.
15. Poverty sometimes causes death by malnutrition.
16. Governments are seldom a cause of low food production.
17. The UNFAO has claimed that many governments reduce food production by discriminating against agriculture.
18. World food production has increased about 10% more than population has grown since 1950.
19. World food production has increased slower than population has grown since 1950.
20. The average world diet has increased by about 400 calories per day since 1960.
21. The average diet in low income and in developing countries has improved by more than 500 calories per day since 1961.
22. Substantially all developing countries by 1990 have made substantial improvements in their per caput food production.
23. The diet in developing countries has improved by about 40% since 1947.
24. The diet in developing countries has steadily deteriorated as population has grown.
25. The U.S. Academy of Sciences said that an average man requires 3,000 calories daily and an average woman needs 2,500 calories daily.
26. In an increasing number of countries an average of less than 2,000 calories are consumed daily.
27. Since 1961, the percentage of people in developing countries consuming less than 2,000 calories per day has decreased from 74% to 6%.

28. Since 1961, the percentage of people in developing countries consuming more than 2,600 calories per day has decreased from 50% to 2%.

29. The amount of grain produced per person has slightly decreased between 1984 and 1990.

30. The amount of grain produced per person has substantially increased since 1983.

31. The amount of grain produced increased 2.6 times from 1950 to 1984.

32. Meat production has been increasing about 1% per year faster than population has grown.

33. Jane Fonda, who spoke against the US effort in Vietnam from Hanoi during the Vietnam War, spoke on population to the UN.

34. The UNFAO alleged that international grain prices fell so far after 1981 and there was such an oversupply of grain that governments had to take steps to reduce grain production.

35. Food production has more than tripled since 1948 with little increase in growing land.

36. Plants grown by only .001% of incoming sunlight are consumed by humans and their animals.

37. Nearly all potential agricultural land is now used to grow food.

38. More land is in forest than in crops on each continent.

39. The world has far more land in forest than in agriculture.

40. With appropriate investment such as fertilizer and irrigation, 90% of the world's land could be used for agriculture.

41. By 1990, people in nearly 90% of the large developing countries ate more calories, on average than necessary for health.

42. People in Bangladesh and India consume on average less than the recommended average of 2200 calories daily.

43. Planned Parenthood fund raising letters have claimed that "Each day 38,000 children perish for lack of food and water."

44. The UNFAO claims that a $1,000.00 machine can process leaves to make nutritious food for humans.

CHAPTER 3—RESOURCES AND ENERGY

45. Paul Ehrlich won a bet that he could predict five resources that would increase in value.

46. Paul Ehrlich bet that he could predict five resources that would increase in value, but instead they decreased by more than 50%.

47. The price of all mineral resources has decreased over the long run.

48. Known reserves decrease as removable resources are used.

49. Once reserves of minerals are used up, they cannot be replaced by other supplies formerly excluded from the reserves.

50. Over short periods of time, reserves always increase.

51. Oil reserves increased to record levels after 1990.

52. Increased oil use meant the reserves after 1990 would not last as many years as reserves before 1990.

53. U.S. oil reserves declined after 1970.

54. For nearly 100 years, the US government predictions about future oil reserves were low by more than 75%.

55. U.S. Government predictions about future US oil reserves have been reasonably accurate.

56. When the U.S. Government said US oil reserves would decrease, they increased, and just after the U.S. Government said the U.S. had vast undiscovered oil deposits many times greater than all previous discoveries in the entire world, U.S. oil reserves decreased.

57. Much oil has cost less than one penny per gallon to discover and produce.

58. Gasoline which sells for a dollar or more per gallon costs at least 50 cents a gallon to discover and produce.

59. The low cost of discovering and producing oil indicates there is plenty left in the ground.

60. Oil field maps indicate most of the earth's surface has already been explored for oil.

61. There is no way an ordinary person can check to see if we are really running out of oil.

62. Natural gas reserves have been about enough for 60 years consumption.

63. Natural gas reserves are growing.

64. Coal reserves are sufficient for hundreds of years.

65. Tidal power will soon be producing enormous amounts of electricity.

66. Over the long run, resources are so plentiful they no longer limit economic decisions.

67. The UN Secretary General said the improvement in the resource situation has been perhaps the most revolutionary man has ever known.

68. Technology has made greater useful output possible with fewer resources.

69. About 90% of water is in the ocean.

70. About 98% of fresh water is frozen into polar ice.

71. There is nearly 100 billion grams of fresh water for every person on earth.

72. Earth's fresh water could cover all the land 13 feet deep.

73. The polar ice is about equal to 1,000 years flow of all rivers and would cover all the land about 100 feet deep.

74. The cost of providing clean water in Africa has increased since the 1980's.

75. Most people in developing countries lack clean water.

76. More populous countries are more likely to have safe water.

77. More crowded countries are more likely to lack safe water.

78. Urban areas are more likely to have clean water.

79. There is no way to substantially reduce the amount of water needed to grow food.

80. Non-agricultural water use can be reduced by about half.

81. The earth receives about 10,000 times as much energy from the sun as we use.

82. 0.2% of sunlight produces the winds, waves, and currents.

83. Plants use about .02% of incoming sunlight.

84. The price of generating electricity from sunlight by solar cells is still too costly for widespread application.

85. Today's cost of generating electricity via solar cells is about 1% of the cost about 20 years ago.

86. There has been no measurable reduction in the amount of oxygen in the air.

87. Tree growth has been reduced by additional CO_2.

CHAPTER 4—EARTH, EMPTY OR CROWDED

88. About half the square kilometers of earth's land surface have no inhabitants.
89. If everyone were put in a big ball, the radius would be about 1/4 mile.
90. Many cities have enough buildings to contain all earth's people.
91. All the earth's people could stand in an area less than 12 miles by 12 miles.
92. Every month spiders eat bugs weighing about as much as all earth's people.
93. About 4% of the US is paved.
94. About 6% of the US is developed.
95. About 1% of earth's land is covered by homes.
96. About 10% of earth's land is used by all farms and cities.
97. If Vermont was almost as crowded as Manhattan, everyone could live there.
98. If everyone lived in the U.S., the U.S. would be as crowded as New Jersey is today.
99. Four story apartments would be required to house everyone in U.S. Government forests.

CHAPTER 5—POPULATION HISTORY, BIRTH RATES, DEATH RATES, DENSITY, GROWTH

100. World population is growing at more than 2% annually.
101. The world population growth percentage rate is increasing.
102. World population growth is expected to decrease.
103. China's population control policy has been associated with the killing of millions of baby girls.
104. Fewer babies are expected to be born after 1999.
105. Fewer babies are being born today in every region except Africa and South Asia.
106. People in China and India are about twice as likely to live under crowded urban conditions as people in Australia and Canada.

CHAPTER 6—EXTINCTION OF SPECIES

107. The U.S. Government Global 2000 Report predicted that in 20 years hundreds of thousands of species would become extinct.
108. The U.S. Government in 1993 confirmed that only 7 species had become extinct in the past 20 years.
109. A subspecies is part, perhaps only a tiny fraction, of a species.
110. Those claiming extinction of massive numbers of species have lied in that they have referred to subspecies as species.
111. There is evidence of massive numbers of species becoming extinct.
112. A subspecies must be at least a substantial fraction of the entire species.
113. A subspecies can be as few as the termites in just one house.

CHAPTER 7—POLLUTION

114. Most of earth's people lack safe water.
115. The U.S. Government NAPAP study found acid rain to be a major problem.
116. Increasing population has caused increased U.S. air pollution.
117. Alar has been found to be a serious cancer risk.
118. Blue asbestos is very harmful.

119. White asbestos cannot be flushed from the lungs.
120. Dioxin is very poisonous to guinea pigs, but not to humans.
121. For every person, there are more than 300 million insects.
122. Noise can kill.
123. Noise can cause permanent hearing loss.
124. U.S. Ozone pollution has decreased.
125. U.S. particulate pollution has increased.
126. Pollution has become worse in modern times.
127. U.S. water pollution has decreased.

CHAPTER 8—GLOBAL WARMING

128. Since 1881, there has been a 0.5 degree Celsius increase in average world temperature.
129. The five hottest years since 1881 were in the 1980s.
130. There was no substantial greenhouse effect until people added to atmospheric CO_2.
131. All major greenhouse gases are increasing.
132. Computer models have predicted a 3 to 5 degree Celsius increase in earth temperature.
133. Atmospheric CO_2 has doubled since pre-industrial times.
134. So far, global warming has been less than predicted by global warming theory.
135. The greenhouse effect global warming theory is supported by most of the evidence.
136. Increase of greenhouse gases near earth's surface substantially decreases energy transport back to outer space.
137. Earth's greenhouse effect is already 93% effective in catching energy radiated toward space by earth's surface.
138. Water makes a vast difference between the greenhouse effects of earth and Venus.
139. Water bypasses the greenhouse effect by evaporating at earth's surface and turning into rain above most greenhouse gases.
140. Most atmosphere scientists claim there has been substantial greenhouse warming since 1881.
141. Greenhouse warming would possibly increase ocean levels.
142. Satellite measurements are the best evidence of earth temperature change.
143. Satellites indicate that earth's temperature has increased by 1/2 degree.
144. The only U.S. warming has occurred near cities since 1920.
145. The U.S. countryside has warmed since 1920.
146. There is no way to determine temperatures before thermometers were invented.
147. The amount the earth has warmed depends on whether you begin and end with a warm year or a cool year.
148. If the starting year is unusually cold, all years you compare to it will seem warmer.
149. 1881 is the first year when temperatures were taken in enough areas to make a reasonable estimate of average earth temperature.
150. The years around 1881 when temperature measurements were first made in many areas were unusually warm.
151. The warming since 1881 cannot be a return to normal.
152. The oceans have absorbed enough heat to disguise global warming.

153. Greenhouse gases interfere with radiation of energy.

154. Radiation is the primary way heat is carried from the surface to the upper atmosphere.

155. Radiation is the only way substantial energy is transmitted from earth to outer space.

156. Convection prevents additional greenhouse gases from substantially warming earth.

157. About 93% of energy from earth's surface is carried to the upper atmosphere by convection, not radiation.

158. The glass of a greenhouse lets in sunlight, but traps higher energy outgoing radiation from the greenhouse interior.

159. The greenhouse effect is caused by some gases letting in sunlight and trapping outgoing radiation.

160. Greenhouse gases trap incoming sunlight to warm the earth.

161. Carbon dioxide (CO_2) is the second most important greenhouse gas.

162. One vapor accounts for 98% of the greenhouse effect.

163. The earth's greenhouse effect can be increased only where there is insignificant water vapor.

164. Outgoing radiation is primarily emitted by CO_2 from about 4 miles above earth's surface.

165. We cannot know where earth's radiation to space comes from.

166. Increasing CO_2 is likely to increase earth's temperature in the high atmosphere, not at the surface.

167. Water vapor is concentrated lower in earth's atmosphere than other gases.

168. Atmosphere CO_2 concentration doubled by 1990.

169. Atmosphere CO_2 will double from today's level by 2050.

170. CO_2 is the major food of plants.

171. More CO_2 makes plants grow more.

172. More CO_2 makes plants need more water.

173. Doubling CO_2 makes some trees grow 3 times as fast.

174. Nothing but conservation can prevent CO_2 from doubling.

175. The more people pollute, the faster the earth warms.

176. A 1991 volcanic eruption increased earth's temperature.

177. Predictions of global warming are based on computer projections.

178. The computer projections of global warming have overcome all criticism.

179. The computers correctly predicted the warming we have had.

180. Earth's temperature increased during the same years that CO_2 was increasing.

181. Earth's temperature has increased about the amount predicted by the computers.

182. Nobody has been able to point to any great errors in the computer models.

183. The computer models accurately consider all major factors related to global warming.

184. The difference between earth's coldest and warmest recent years is about one degree Celsius.

185. Most global warming was before there was significant CO_2 increase.

186. The warming is in the wrong places to be caused by CO_2 increase.

187. Change in solar activity correlates very well with the warming since 1881.

CHAPTER 9—OZONE

188. Ozone is an energetic form of O_2 .

189. Ultraviolet radiation is similar to visible light, except it is higher in wavelength and energy.

190. Ozone high in the atmosphere absorbs ultraviolet B radiation.

191. It has been proven that freon destroys ozone high in the atmosphere.

192. The ozone hole has gradually increased in size as atmosphere freon concentrations have increased.

193. Ultraviolet B radiation at earth's surface has increased in proportion to decrease in ozone.

194. We know the ozone hole did not exist before freons were invented.

195. There are changes in high atmosphere ozone concentration of at least 50% for reasons we do not understand.

196. About 1980, the National Academy of Sciences predicted that ozone depletion would be 9%.

197. About 1980, the National Academy of Sciences predicted that ozone depletion would be 3%.

198. About 1980, the National Academy of Sciences predicted that ozone depletion would be 18%.

199. There are 3 intensities of ultraviolet radiation, called A, B, and C.

200. Ultraviolet C is the most energetic ultraviolet radiation and makes ozone.

201. Ozone is the only gas in the atmosphere that stops ultraviolet B radiation.

202. Ultraviolet B radiation affects the entire earth about equally.

203. The ozone hole is over the Antarctic, so the Antarctic receives more ultraviolet B radiation than the equator.

204. The equator receives about 50 times as much ultraviolet B radiation as the Antarctic.

205. Freon is stable in the lower atmosphere but is broken up by ultraviolet radiation in the upper atmosphere.

206. Less than 10,000 tons of freon are in the upper atmosphere.

207. Billions of tons of ozone are formed every second in the upper atmosphere.

208. In the lower atmosphere, ozone has a half life of seconds to minutes.

209. In the upper atmosphere, ozone has a half life of days to months.

210. Mt. Erebus, a volcano in Antarctica releases large amounts of chlorine into the atmosphere.

211. Large volcanic eruptions have been followed by a decrease in atmosphere ozone levels.

212. The ozone hole forms about May when the sun sets for the Antarctic winter.

213. The ozone hole dissipates about September when the sun rises for the Antarctic summer.

214. The ozone hole forms over the Antarctic, not the Arctic.

215. Wind patterns permit the ozone hole to form.

CHAPTER 10—QUALITY OF LIFE

216. UNICEF lists about 20 statistics related to quality of life, and most are better in less crowded areas.

217. The UN Statistical Yearbook lists more than 20 statistics related to quality of life, and all are better in more crowded areas.
218. As population has grown, most measures of quality of life have deteriorated.
219. Measures of quality of life are on average much better in more populated countries.
220. Measures of quality of life are on average all worse in less densely populated countries.
221. Measures of quality of life are usually better in less crowded parts of countries.
222. The most important measure of quality of life has deteriorated during the time of the population explosion.
223. During the time of the population explosion, quality of life has improved at the fastest rate in history.
224. During the population explosion since 1945, infant mortality has halved.
225. During the population explosion, life expectancy has doubled in developing countries.
226. During the population explosion, the number of children starting school has increased to more than 75%.
227. Most people immigrate toward less crowded areas.
228. By each of nine measures, population growth is associated with a higher quality of life.

Answers and references to reasons why the answers are correct .

1. f	34. t 222	67. t 326	100. f 506	133. f 801	166. t 820	199. t 910	
2. t 102	35. t 224	68. t 328	101. f 506	134. t 802	167. t 821	200. t 911	
3. t 103	36. f 225	69. f 329	102. t 506	135. f 803	168. f 822	201. f 912	
4. f 105	37. f 226	70. t 329	103. t 508	136. f 803	169. f 823	202. f 914	
5. t 113	38. f 226	71. t 329	104. t 515	137. t 803	170. f 824	203. f 914	
6. f 114	39. t 226	72. t 329	105. t 515	138. t 803	171. t 824	204. t 914	
7. f 201	40. f 227	73. f 329	106. f 521	139. t 803	172. f 824	205. t 918	
8. f 207	41. t 228	74. f 330	107. t 608	140. f 804	173. t 824	206. t 918	
9. t 207	42. f 228	75. f 331	108. t 603	141. t 805	174. f 824	207. t 918	
10. t 209	43. t 229	76. t 331	109. t 618	142. t 806	175. f 825	208. f 919	
11. t 209	44. t 230	77. f 331	110. t 619	143. f 806	176. f 826	209. f 919	
12. f 211	45. f 304	78. t 331	111. f 616	144. t 808	177. t 827	210. t 920	
13. f 211	46. t 304	79. f 334	112. f 620	145. f 808	178. f 828	211. t 923	
14. f 212	47. t 305	80. t 335	113. t 620	146. f 809	179. f 828	212. f 922	
15. t 212	48. f 306	81. t 336	114. f 331	147. t 810	180. f 828	213. f 922	
16. f 213	49. f 306	82. t 336	115. f 701	148. t 810	181. f 828	214. t 922	
17. t 213	50. f 307	83. t 336	116. f 702	149. t 811	182. f 828	215. t 922	
18. f 215	51. t 308	84. f 337	117. f 704	150. f 812	183. f 828	216. f 1002	
19. f 215	52. f 308	85. t 337	118. t 705	151. f 812	184. t 829	217. t 1002	
20. t 216	53. t 309	86. t 338	119. f 705	152. f 813	185. t 831	218. f 1002	
21. t 216	54. t 311	87. f 339	120. t 710	153. t 814	186. t 832	219. t 1002	
22. t 217	55. f 311	88. t 405	121. t 717	154. f 814	187. t 833	220. t 1002	
23. t 217	56. t 311	89. t 407	122. t 719	155. t 814	188. f 901	221. f 1002	
24. f 217	57. t 317	90. t 407	123. t 719	156. t 814	189. f 902	222. f 1003	
25. f 218	58. f 318	91. t 409	124. t 720	157. t 815	190. t 903	223. t 1004	
26. t 219	59. t 318	92. t 410	125. f 722	158. f 817	191. f 905	224. t 1004	
27. t 219	60. f 319	93. f 411	126. f 725	159. t 816	192. f 905	225. f 1004	
28. f 219	61. f 321	94. f 412	127. t 732	160. f 817	193. f 905	226. t 1004	
29. t 222	62. t 322	95. f 413	128. t 801	161. t 818	194. f 905	227. f 1006	
30. t 222	63. t 322	96. t 415	129. t 801	162. t 818	195. t 907	228. t 1106	
31. t 222	64. t 323	97. t 416	130. f 801	163. t 819	196. t 908		
32. t 222	65. f 324	98. f 419	131. f 801	164. f 819	197. t 908		
33. t 222	66. t 326	99. f 420	132. t 801	165. f 820	198. t 908		

APPENDIX-UNIT CONVERSION TABLE

Length
Centimeter 1/2.54 inches, 1/100 meters
foot   12 inches, 1/3 yard, 30.5 cm, .305 m, 1/5280 mi
inch   1/12 foot, 0.083 feet, 2.54 cm, 1/39.37 m,
kilometer 1,000 meters, .621 miles (between 3/5 and 5/8)
meter   100 cm, 1.093 yards, 39.37 inches, 1/1,000 km
micron   1/1,000,000 meter, 0.0000394 inches
mile   5280 ft, 1760 yds, 1.61 km, 63,360 inches
mile, nautical 1.852 km, 1.151 miles
yard   0.914 meters, 36 inches, 3 feet, 1/1760 miles

Area
Acre   0.404 hectares, 43,560 ft^2, 4,840 yds^2, 1/640 mi^2
$foot^2$ 929 cm^2, 144 in^2, 1/27,878,400 mi^2
hectare   10,000 $meters^2$, 2.471 acres, 1/100 km^2, 1/259 mi^2
km^2 100 hectares, 247 acres, .386 $miles^2$, 1,000,000m^2
$meter^2$ 10,000 cm^2, 1/10,000 hectare, 1.196 yd^2,
$mile^2$ 259 hectares, 2.59 km^2, 640 acres, 27,878,400 ft^2
$yard^2$ 0.836 $meters^2$, 1296 in^2, 9 $feet^2$

Volume
Barrel   42 Gallons, about 300 lbs petroleum, 159 liters, 7.33
           barrels/metric ton, .136 metric tons
$foot^3$ .028 m^3, 1,728 in^3, 1/27 $yard^3$,
gallon   3.786 liters, 4 quarts, 1/42 barrel, 231 in^3
liter   0.001 $meters^3$, 61 $inches^3$, 1.057 quarts, liquid
$meter^3$ 1.000 liter, 1.308 yd^3, 1,000,000 cm^3, 35.3 ft^3
quart, liquid 0.946 liters, 2 liquid pints, 1/4 gallon
$yard^3$ 0.765 $meters^3$, 27 $feet^3$

Mass
gram   1/1,000 kilograms, .039 ounces, 1/453.6 lbs
kilogram 0.001 metric tons, 2.205 lbs, 1000 grams, 35.3 oz
ounce, av 28.350 grams, 1/16 pounds, 1/35.3 kg
pound, av 16 ounces, 453.6 grams, 1/2.2 kg, 1/2,000 tons
ton, metric, 1,000 kg, 2,205 lbs
ton, short,   970.2 kg, 2,000 lbs

Energy and Heat
BTU   1,054 joules, 252 calories
calorie   .00397 BTU, 4.184 joules
joule   0.738 ft lbs, 0.239 calories, 0.000949 BTU, 10,000,000
           ergs, 1 amp over 1 ohm for 1 second
degrees   Celsius, multiply by 1.8 and add 32 to get degrees F
           Fahrenheit, subtract 32 and divide by 1.8 to get degrees C
watt (power) 1J/sec, 0.738 ft lbs/sec

INDEX

NOTES

NOTES